THE HISTORY OF BEER IN AMERICA

THE HISTORY OF
BEER IN AMERICA

AN AGS BookWorks Book

Produced by
AGS BookWorks
PO Box 460313
San Francisco, California 94146
www.agsbookworks.com

Designed by Bill Yenne

Printed in China

ABOUT THE AUTHOR

Bill Yenne is the San Francisco-based author of
more than three dozen books on a wide variety of
historical topics from Lewis and Clark to the
American aviation industry. *The Wall Street Journal*
recently said of his work that it "has the rare quality of being both an excellent reference work and a
pleasure to read." The reviewer also wrote that Mr.
Yenne writes with "cinematic vividness."
He has appeared on the History Channel to discuss
the history of beer. He has also been a featured
guest on Beer Radio. Once referred to by brewpub
pioneer Buffalo Bill Owens as "the American
Michael Jackson" (the king of English beverage historians, not the king of pop), Mr. Yenne has written
extensively on beer and brewing history for two
decades.

Among his beer books are: *The American
Brewery, Great American Beers: Twelve Brands That
Became Icons, Beers of North America, Beers of the
World*, and *Beer Labels of the World*, as well as *The
Field Guide To Breweries and Microbreweries of North
America.*

Mr. Yenne has also contributed articles to *All
About Beer Magazine* and has hosted numerous beer
tastings throughout the Unites States. He was a
member of an elite panel chosen to select the beers
to compliment each course of a formal dinner held
at the Oldenberg Brewery. Afterward, Jay Maeder
of *The New York Daily News* described his choice of
a beer to accompany the entree of "Soused and
Stuffed Chicken Breast Marinated in Mustard
Sauce" as "perfect."

ACKNOWLEDGEMENTS:

During more than two decades of writing
about beer and brewing, the author is indebted to
many people within the industry who have shared
their time and resources. Fritz Maytag, Dave
Burkhart and Mark Carpenter at Anchor Brewing
come to mind as having been extremely generous
with their time through the years. Others who have
been more than helpful include Vickie Feese, Tice
Nichols and Jeff Waalkes of Miller Brewing, as well
as Dan Gordon and Dana Kemberling of Gordon
Biersch.

People such as Mark Ruedrich and Tom Allen
of North Coast Brewing and Don Shook of Adolph
Coors have provided valuable material through the
years. Thanks also to John Smallshaw for his con-
sultation regarding Falstaff history; and to Walter
"Terry" Liebman of Rheingold Brewing, who kindly
shared both memorabilia and recollections.

For supplying recent photos for this book, I'd
especially like to thank Adrian Matthew, the
Brand Activist Man for New Belgium Brewing;
Carl Miller at Beerbooks.com; Wendy Tucciarone
of the Kona Brewing Company; Becca Alexander
at Boulevard Brewing and Trent Tokos of Widmer Brothers Brewing, who arranged for me to
use the wonderful Damian Conrad photos of the
brothers.

I have learned a great deal about the beer
more ancient than that of George Washington from
Alan Eames, the late beer archeologist. An inter-
nationally recognized beer expert and importer,
Charles Finkel, has been a good friend and a tire-
less champion of beer as part of the currency of
civilized society. A special nod of thanks is
deserved by Allan Paul of San Francisco Brewing
for his extraordinary beer and continuing great
generosity over many years.

Page one photograph: Three Americans enjoy their
favorite American beers. (*Collection of the author*)

Page two photograph: Craft brewing pioneer Rob
Widmer pours a glass of Hefeweizen at Widmer
Brothers Brewing in Portland, Oregon. (*Damian
Conrad photo, courtesy of Trent Tokos, Widmer Broth-
ers Brewing*)

TABLE OF CONTENTS

CHAPTER 1: EARLY AMERICAN BEER 6

CHAPTER 2: THE LAGER BREWERS ARRIVE 22

CHAPTER 3: BREWING BECOMES A MAJOR AMERICAN INDUSTRY 36

CHAPTER 4: INTO THE TWENTIETH CENTURY 64

CHAPTER 5: NATIONAL BEERS AND REGIONAL FAVORITES 84

CHAPTER 6: AMERICAN BREWERY RENAISSANCE 114

GLOSSARY 144

APPENDICES 154

INDEX 157

EARLY AMERICAN BEER

AMERICANS HAVE BEEN BREWING and enjoying beer for centuries. When Europeans arrived, they observed that the people in both North America and South America drank various corn-based beers known by such names as tizwin or tesguino. In the July 1894 issue of *American Anthropologist*, Captain John G. Bourke quoted Columbus as having observed people drinking tizwin. Perhaps he tried it himself. Bourke discusses the people of Veragua on the coast of Central America using corn to make tizwin. He also notes a dissimilar corn-meal sour beverage that was enjoyed by the Cherokee in North America. Of tizwin, Bourke went on to say that "this spicy drink resembling English Beer was also a drink of the Arizona Apaches, their sacred intoxicant."

In what we now call the American Southwest, corn-based beer had existed long before the first Europeans set foot in that region. For the people who lived in the plateaus and canyons of this vast territory, the corn was a dual purpose cereal grain. Once stockpiled in a corn crib, it could either be eaten or used for making the beer. This was a common paradigm in the ancient world. For example, the Sumerians baked barley loaves called "bappir" that could be stored in the dry climate and either eaten as bread or mixed with malted barley to form a mash for brewing.

In his 1907 book *The North American Indian*, Edward Curtis described the making of tizwin: "It is, in fact, a yeast beer. In preparing it, corn is first soaked in water. If it be winter time the wet corn is placed under a sleeping blanket until the warmth of the body causes it to sprout; if summer, it is deposited in a shallow hole, covered with a wet blanket, and left until the sprouts appear, when it is ground to pulp on a metate. Water and roots are added, and the mixture is boiled and strained to remove the coarser roots and sprouts. At this stage the liquid has the consistency of thin cream soup. It is now set aside for twenty-four hours to cool and ferment, when it is fit for drinking. . . . Used in moderation it is not a bad beverage."

In northern Mexico, tesguino is still being brewed in the old ways by the Tarahumara (they call themselves Raramuri) people. In a recent interview for National Public Radio, John Burnett spoke with Guadalupe Espino Palma, the Raramuri governor of the Norogachi district. Palma explained that "God taught the Raramuri how to make corn beer. We make offerings of tesguino to God himself, and He drinks it also. We use tesguino for dancing, and we enjoy drinking it."

Beer and brewing have been part of civilization since antiquity. It has been suggested that the brewing of beer is at least as old as the baking of bread, and certainly both have been practiced since the dawn of recorded history. Professor Solomon Katz at the University of Pennsylvania has found Sumerian recipes for beer that date back four millennia, and beer is mentioned often in ancient Egyptian literature. As H.F. Lutz points out in *Viticulture and Brewing in the Ancient Orient*, Middle Kingdom texts from Beni Hasan "enumerate quite a number of different beers." Among these a "garnished beer" and a "dark beer." As David Ryder points out in the *Newsletter of the American Society of Brewing Chemists*, Egyptian beer "was also used as a medicine, a tonic for building strength. . . a universal cure for coughs and colds, shortness of breath, problems of the stomach and lungs, and a guard against indigestion!"

Beer and brewing evolved as civilization evolved. Beer is mentioned by Xenophon and Aristotle (as quoted by Athenaeus). Among others, the Roman consul and scholar Pliny the Younger estimated that nearly 200 types of beer were being brewed in Europe by the first century. The Latin texts refer to the barley bev-

Opposite and above: **Some of the earliest regular brewing activities in what is now the United States occurred more than a thousand years ago in places such as Wupatki in Arizona and Mesa Verde in Colorado.** *(National Park Service)*

Chapter Three

The Beer in the Ancient Orient

Peoples in all ages and climates have prepared naturally fermented beverages from any available material. The statement of Pliny [1] "if any one will take the trouble duly to consider the matter, he will find that upon no one subject is the industry of man kept more constantly on the alert than upon the making of wine", can be augmented by the addition "and of beer". The brewing industry in its beginnings in historic times was a home industry like that of baking bread. Indeed the work of the baker and that of the brewer was very much alike in the initial stages of brewing. The earliest Egyptian texts enumerate quite a number of different beers. One of the oldest generic terms for beer seems to be *sehpet*, Shpt-beer Pyr. Texts W 143 a; T 114 a; N 451 a; Beni Hasan I, pl. 17 etc. On the stele of Khabiousokari in the Museum of Cairo a certain beer is called *hn-*. In the pyramid-texts we meet with a "dark beer", an "iron beer" and the *hes*-beer, i. e., "garnished beer" [2]. The pyramid-texts further mention the *ph*-beer, (W 144 a; T 115 a; N 452 a, which is probably the same as the *ph*-beer, in Beni Hasan I, pl. 17), the -beer (W 141 a; T 112 a; N 449 a) and the beer of Nubia, *hk.t sty*, (W 145 a; T 116 a; N 453 a). Under the rubrique *sehpet*, "beer", are also mentioned very early the

1) Pliny, XIV, 22.
2) See Lutz, 46, 53, 54, 55.

The beer in the Ancient Orient. 73

beverages (probably identical with the beverage called and *pzte*, . The former only is found again by Hathorneferhotep in the same category, but there it is again mentioned under the heading of *hrw.t*, and of *nms.t*, . Probably these latter two names refer also to certain kinds of beer [1]. *Nms.t* may possibly be connected with the name for cellar, *nmte*, as the designation of a beverage, which was kept in the cellar. In the Egyptian bazaar-scene [2], dating back to the fifth dynasty, the second row shows a woman offering for sale a beverage, which bears the name *nmst*, , to a man, who kneels before a perfume vase. The woman is saying to him, "It is *nmst* that satisfies thee", . The liquor is contained in two white bowls, which she extends towards the prospective buyer. This market-scene is of interest, since it shows that even at that early time liquors were sold by women in public places. In Dümichen, *Kal. Inschr.*, 46, 1 appears a certain kind of beer, called "friend's-beer" or, "beer of the protector" or Beni Hasan I, pl. 17; *hk.t hnms*, which was probably an old beer, or lager-beer. Sweet beer is mentioned, f. i., in Med,

1) Weil, Raymond, *Des monuments et de l'histoire des IIe et IIIe dynasties*, Paris, 1908, pp. 249 and 253.
2) The *nmte* is a cellar in which any kind of beverages were stored: The beer-cellar proper was called Journ. Asiat., 1867, p. 449.
3) LD II, 96 and Maspero, *Bibliothèque Égyptologique*, VIII, (1900) plate facing p. 250. On the element beverage, see above, p. 79, n. 1.
4) Mistake for *pzte*,

Above: **For his** *Viticulture and Brewing in the Ancient Orient,* **H.F. Lutz researched ancient Egyptian brewing in minute detail.** *Right:* **From Lutz's book, a "scene after the close of a banquet."** *(Collection of the author)*

erages as cerevisia or cerevisium, root words that are still with us in the Spanish and Portuguese words for beer — cerveza and cerveja — as well as in the latin name for brewer's yeast, *saccharomyces cerevisiae.*

When Europeans first came to North America to stay, they brought both beer and brewers. Beer was imported into the London Company's Jamestown Colony in Virginia within a few months of its being established in 1607, and records show that the company was planning for brewers to be sent to the colony in 1609. Farther north, beer came over on the *Mayflower* — although the crew kept this beer for the trip home. Running short of supplies, they dropped the pilgrims at Plymouth, instead of the mouth of the Hudson as planned, and headed for home. According to Edward Winslow, author of *Mourt's Relation: A Journal of the Pilgrims at Plymouth, 1622:* "We could not now take time for further search or consideration, our victuals being much spent, especially our beer."

The pilgrims who had been left without beer when the *Mayflower* turned home are recorded to have craved it, but not to have brewed it. Even the straight-laced Puritans, who established the nearby Massachusetts Bay Colony a few years later, described beer not as sinful, but as essential. The Puritan minister Richard Mather, grandfather of the firebrand fundamentalist, Cotton Mather, wrote in 1635 of "wholesome beere."

Neither barley nor commercially-grown hops were widely available initially, so the early seventeenth century brewers made do with what they had. The Dutch in North America are believed to have made use of indigenous wild hops before the English, who used spruce as a bittering agent in place of hops. The English, like the Indians of the Southwest, used corn instead of barley as a fermentable starch. In this sense, the early beer produced by the Massachusetts brewers had more in common with the tesguino of the pueblos than it did with London ale. By the end of the seventeenth century, however, barley was well established as one of New England's key cash crops.

Breweries were established within what is now the United States in the seventeenth century, although no one is sure of the date or location of the first European brewery. However, historical records show that several were in operation around Massachusetts Bay and in Virginia by the 1630s. One of the earliest Massachusetts brewers mentioned by name was Robert

Sedgewick, who was active in Charlestown by this time.

The Massachusetts Bay Colony began permitting taverns to brew their own beer, and the first Boston brewpub opened in 1639. Today, an institution that often exists in proximity to a brewpub is a college. America's first such institution, Harvard College (now Harvard University) in Cambridge was founded in 1636. Within a few years, Harvard probably had a brewpub nearby, but it is most remarkable for having had its own on-campus brewery by at least 1674 and possibly as early as 1667. Harvard would continue to make beer routinely available to its students for more than a century, but the practice eventually faded. The last of three Harvard brewhouses was destroyed in 1814 — burned down by underclassmen.

The first major center of commercial brewing in North America was in New Amsterdam on Manhattan Island, in a Dutch, rather than English colony. The Netherlands West India Company established its first two North American colonies in 1623, with the settlement on Manhattan coming several years later. The West India Company built the first commercial brewery in New Amsterdam in 1632 on what came to be known as

Brouwerstraat (Brewer's Street, now Stone Street). The term "Manhattan beer" soon became synonymous with beer of high quality. By the end of the decade breweries proliferated throughout New Amsterdam, to other sites along the Hudson River to the north and throughout the colony of New Netherlands. One of the earliest New Amsterdam breweries was operated by Balthazar Bayard, and his brothers Nicholas and Peiter, all nephews of Peter Stuyvesant, the governor of New Netherlands.

America's first name-brand beer was brewed by the Red Lion Brewery, which was located just north of present-day Wall Street. Founded in 1660 by Isaac de Forest, it survived until 1675, when it was destroyed by fire.

Located between the English colonies in Virginia and Massachusetts, New Amsterdam quickly became one of the key trading cities in North America. In 1664, it also became English. The Duke of York (later King James II) intimidated Peter Stuyvesant into surrendering New Netherlands without a shot being fired. New Amsterdam was then promptly renamed in honor of the Duke. The political changes seem not to have disturbed the brewing activities in the slightest, and the Dutch

Left: The Pabst Brewing Company of Milwaukee ran this ad in the 1890s, celebrating the "Perfection" of American brewing with a nod to one of the earliest vessels to bring beer to American shores. (*Collection of the author*)

Above left: **Peter Stuyvesant, New Amsterdam's founding father was also the father of two of its earliest brewers.** *Above:* **Downtown New Amsterdam contained both taverns and breweries.** *(Collection of the author)*

brewers missed not a beat as their city became New York. Indeed, the English soon supported the brewing industry by levying taxes on wine and rum, while exempting beer and cider that was produced in the colonies.

Meanwhile, there were small breweries cropping up throughout English-speaking North America from Rhode Island to Georgia. William Penn, the founder of Pennsylvania, like many of his fellow Quakers, was fond of beer and featured it prominently in his famous 1683 treaty with the Indians. It was at about this same time that Penn built a 700-square-foot brewery on his own estate near Bristol. Although his house soon burned down, the Penn brewery survived until 1864 — nearly two centuries later.

In the same year that Penn built his brewhouse, William Frampton, a Quaker from New York started the first commercial brewery in Philadelphia. It was located on Front Street near Dock Street in Pennsylvania's chief port and largest city. It would take eight decades, but the brewer's

art finally crossed the Alleghenies in 1765, when the first brewery in the West was built by His Majesty's army at Fort Pitt, today's Pittsburgh.

Philadelphia soon emerged second only to New York as an American brewing center. Among the more important brewers, the Emlens were a prosperous Quaker merchant family who supplied beer throughout the city for at least three generations. Located on Fifth Street, the Emlen Brewery also provided sustenance for ships that were fitting out in Philadelphia's harbor.

Neighborhood breweries and brewpubs, all small-scale operations, remained important in Philadelphia as well. One such place where beer was served — and probably brewed — was the colorfully-named Man Full o' Trouble Tavern. Built in 1759, it was operated by Michael Sisk until 1773, when James Alexander took over to guide it through the Revolutionary period. Martha Smallwood became the first woman publican at the site in 1796. The establishment was later known as Stafford's Tavern, the Cove Cornice House and Naylor's Hotel.

Among the more interesting eighteenth century establishments was the Three Tun Tavern at Mount Holly, New

Jersey. Built by Samuel Briant before 1737, it had a name that clearly confirms that brewing beer was an important activity. Indeed, if three lauter tuns were present, the quantity of beer being produced would have been substantial. Through the years, the tavern and its inn had numerous famous patrons. During the American Revolution, Lord Cornwallis occupied rooms at the Three Tun. The name was changed to the Square & Compass in early in the nineteenth century and in 1805 it became a meeting place of the Masonic order. In 1825 it was renamed as the Sign of General Jackson after Andrew Jackson. During prohibition, the establishment became the Mill Street Hotel.

By the early eighteenth century, brewing had spread beyond the Northeast and Virginia. In Baltimore, the first major brewery seems to have been started in 1748 by Elias Daniel Barnitz and his brother John. While John dropped out after a year, Elias remained involved with the company for more than three decades. In the South, Major William Horton constructed a brewery at Jekyll Island, Georgia in 1738, and the Single brothers established a brewery at Salem, North Carolina in 1774. By this time, other breweries were noted along the Mississippi River and well beyond the colonies that would form the original 13 states. In 1765, a brewery was established at the French colonial settlement of Kaskaskia in what is now Illinois.

Beer in colonial times would have been clearly recognizable to a twenty-first century beer-lover. Eighteenth century English and colonial ale was an amber-colored, lightly-hopped, bottom-fermenting beer similar to modern English ale, or today's craft-brewed American ale. As in all beer, then as now, the shade of the amber color was relative to the extent to which the malted barley was roasted. While barley is the definitive malting grain in beer-making, the English occasionally used oats, and the American colonists sometimes made do with corn and wheat.

Above: **Enjoying some frivolity in a colonial ale house. (*Collection of the author*)**

Colonial ale was occasionally flavored as in contemporary Belgian-style fruit beers. Letters and documents dating from the colonial period indicate that eighteenth century brewers experimented with apple and pumpkin beer, styles that have been revived by modern American craft brewers. India Pale Ale, the beer that was invented by English brewers specifically to

Left: William Penn, brewer, beer advocate and founder of Pennsylvania. *(Collection of the author) Below:* The legendary Man Full o' Trouble Tavern was established in Philadelphia in 1759. *(Library of Congress)*

be exported to English colonists in India, was also exported to the American colonies. It was higher in alcohol, and extra hops were added as a preservative to help sustain the beer for the long ocean journey. Refrigeration, other than to pack something in ice, did not exist in the eighteenth century, and ice could not survive a trip to India.

In colonial times, large commercial breweries as we know them did not yet exist. The brewing industry involved local brewers whose radius of distribution was analogous to that of the local bakery. A village brewer would usually brew for the village, or, in the case of a city, for the narrow confines of the neighborhood or a portion of the city. A maltster, on the other hand, might supply malt for a number of brewers over a wider radius. Even as larger commercial breweries began operations in the cities, taverns would continue to routinely brew their own beer throughout the eighteenth century.

As with many industries, brewing and malting were family businesses. In New York City, the Rutgers family — the Dutch ancestors of the Colonel Henry Rutgers who endowed the university of the same name in 1825 — had emerged as the city's most important brewers. The Rutgers

Brewery was located on Stone Street, as the English had renamed the street known as Brouwerstraat when the Dutch owned Manhattan. One of many breweries in the city, the Rutgers establishment would be a fixture in lower Manhattan throughout the eighteenth century until it was destroyed by fire in 1783.

Joseph Adams, a maltster in Braintree, Massachusetts in the 1690s, was the patriarch of a long line of descendants that included his great-grandson, the famous revolutionary, Samuel Adams of Boston.

Just as beer and brewing were integral parts of life in the colonies in the eighteenth century, the colonial brewing industry was an integral part of the movement toward independence and the revolution in which Sam Adams played such a role. The same draconian tax laws that eventually led to such signature protests as the Boston Tea Party might just as well have led to a Boston *Beer* Party — although beer, unlike tea, originated locally.

After the costly French & Indian War ended in 1763, the British government attempted to raise money for colonial defense through a series of taxes on the colonists. First came the short-lived Stamp Act, passed 1765 and repealed a year later. Next came the more wide-ranging Town-shend Acts, which were passed by the English Parliament in 1767. These called for taxation that cut deeply into the lives and pocket books of the colonists with taxes on everything from beer to tea.

One of the leading protesters against these taxes, Sam Adams was to also be a leader of the group of colonists who disguised themselves as Indians and boarded the British tea ships in Boston harbor on the dark night of December 16, 1773.

Meanwhile, two of the towering figures in the revolution of 1776, and in the new nation born of the Declaration of Independence signed that year, were also prominent early American brewers. Both George Washington, and his fellow Virginia aristocrat Thomas Jefferson, were the founding fathers of both America and of American brewing.

Though Washington was a Virginian, he is best remembered as an aficionado of Philadelphia beer. It is well known that he patronized a Philadelphia brewer named Benjamin Morris, and that he favored the porter brewed by Robert Hare, also of

Above: Clearly, a lot of beer was brewed at the appropriately named Three Tun Tavern, which operated as a brewpub in Mount Holly, New Jersey from about 1737. (*Library of Congress*)

Left: **This famous American home brewer was also an advocate of Philadelphia-brewed porter. And, by the way, he was the first president of the United States.** *Below*: **George Washington's grist mill, essential to brewing, near Mount Vernon.** *(Library of Congress)*

Philadelphia. An expatriate Englishman, Hare is believed to have been the first American brewer to produce this smooth dark style of beer that originated in 1722 with London brewer Ralph Harwood. In London, Harwood's creamy invention had quickly became popular with tradesmen — especially porters on the Thames docks.

Meanwhile in Philadelphia, Robert Hare began brewing porter in the auspicious year of 1776. Forced to temporarily abandon the city during the subsequent British occupation, Hare is said to have taken refuge in Virginia. It is possible that he may have had some contact during this time with George Washington, although the general would have been away fighting the Revolutionary War most of the time.

Washington had certainly become acquainted with Hare's porter by 1788, because, on July 20 of that year, he wrote to Clement Biddle, "I beg you will send me a gross of Mr. Hare's best bottled porter if the price is not much enhanced by the copious droughts you took of it at the late procession."

The adjective "best" clearly describes the president's opinion of Hare's product. Two years later, when Washington was at Federal Hall in New York, he asked his secretary, Tobias Lear, to place an order. "Will you be so good as to desire Mr. Hare to have if he continues to make the best porter in Philadelphia, three gross of his best put up for Mount Vernon?" queried Lear, "As the President means to visit that place in the recess of Congress and it is probable there will be a large demand for porter at that time."

As young George Washington was building his career as a surveyor and Army officer, the Emlen family had become an important brewing dynasty in Philadelphia. It is little wonder that in 1777, before moving into winter quarters at nearby Valley Forge, George Washington had his headquarters at the home of George Emlen III. One can imagine the general and his gracious host quaffing mugs of fresh beer.

We can take a peek into the general's eating and drinking habits through a receipt issued to Washington and his entourage in July 1782 by George Evans at Philadelphia's City Tavern. In addition to showing three dinners on July 21, five breakfasts on July 23, two breakfasts and four "gentleman's breakfasts" on July 24, it states that "There were punch and beverages, beer and cider and three bottles of wine for the sick included."

During the American Revolution, Washington was a constant champion of the beer ration that he felt was deserved by his men. One finds repeated references to beer and the beer ration in his personal papers, which are preserved in the Library of Congress and elsewhere. For example, on July 19, 1777, General Washington wrote to the Continental Congress Army Committee, stating that "With respect to Food, considering we are in such an extensive and abundant Country, No Army was ever worse supplied than ours with many essential Articles of it. Our Soldiers, the greatest part of the last Campaign, and the whole of this, have scarcely tasted any kind of Vegetables, had but little Salt, and Vinegar. Neither have they been provided with proper drink. Beer or Cyder seldom comes within the verge of the Camp, and Rum in much too small quantities."

On July 25, Congress resolved that the committee be empowered to contract for, among other things, "beer, cider and sauerkraut." A few weeks later, on August 5, 1777, Washington wrote to the Continental Congress War Board, that "It does not appear that any person has yet undertaken the Business of Supplying the Army with Beer, or Cyder, Vinegar and Vegeta-

Above: **Might the Boston Tea Party have been the Boston Beer Party? People were angry about those taxes as well.** *(Collection of the author)*

To Make Small Beer by George Washington

Though he favored the porter that was brewed by Robert Hare of Philadelphia, the "Father of Our Country" was also a noted home brewer in his own right, and he made sufficient quantities for his own use and for the entertainment of his guests. In his notebook for the year 1757, he jotted down this recipe for small beer:

Take a large Sifter full of Bran Hops to your Taste — Boil these 3 hours then strain out 30 Gallons. Into a Cooler put in 3 Gallons Molasses while the Beer is scalding hot or rather drain the molasses into the Cooler. Strain the Beer on it while boiling hot let this stand til it is little more than Blood warm. Then put in a quart of Yeast if the weather is very cold cover it over with a Blanket — & Let it work in the Cooler 24 hours then put it into the Cask — leave the Bung open til it is almost done working — Bottle it that day Week it was Brewed.

Above: On August 8, 1775, General George Washington ordered that the ration of provisions allowed by the Continental Congress for each soldier should include "One quart of Spruce Beer per man, per diem, or 9 Gallons of molasses." (*Library of Congress*)

Above right: Issued at Lexington, General George Washington's general orders for January 26, 1778 stated that "The Commander in Chief is pleased to . . . order that. . . the troops should be provided with strong beer at two shillings and sixpence per quart and common beer at one shilling per quart." (*Library of Congress*)

bles; but as those things would exceedingly refresh the Troops that now lay at German Town, I beg to know whether they could not be procured for them immediately, by some person appointed by the Board for the present. If only Beer or Cyder and Vinegar was procured, it would not be so material as to Vegetables, for they can purchase them in the Neighbourhood."

On wintry January 26, 1778, Washington's general orders for the day stated that "The Commander in Chief is pleased to . . . order that. . . [a] Brigade Sutler be appointed, and liquors sold at the following prices and under the following regulations: Peach brandy by the quart at 7/6 by the Pint 4/, by the Gill 1/3. Whiskey and Apple brandy at 6/ pr. quart, 3/6 pr. pint and 1/ by the gill. Cyder at 1/3 by the quart; Strong beer 2/6 by the quart. Common beer 1/ by the quart." (The prices are in schillings and pence.)

George Washington eventually decided that the Continental Army should under-

write the cost of beer for the troops. In a letter to Alexander Hamilton, penned on May 2, 1783, he wrote that "If spruce, or any other kind of small beer, could be provided, it ought to be given gratis, but not made part of the Compact with [the troops]."

For Washington, porter also had a political dimension. After the war, the first president was a champion of the notion that Americans should buy the products of American manufacturers rather than purchasing goods that were imported from England. Porter was specifically mentioned. Washington was quick to point out that he bought only "American porter" and asked that his fellow countrymen follow his example.

By the 1760s, and probably sooner, bottled British porter began to be exported, first to Ireland, and then to the American colonies. In Ireland, however, a number of brewers began making porter, not the least of whom was Arthur Guinness, who began brewing at the Saint James's Gate Brewery in Dublin in 1759. Eventually, Irish porter would become a global gold standard in non-golden beer, and Guinness would be the crown jewel. The Guinness operation at Saint James's Gate would later become the largest brewery in the world. In the twenty-first century, Guinness Stout, originally "stout porter," remains the largest selling beer in the world that is not a pale yellow lager.

In the quieter years before the war and after his presidency, Washington had brewed his own at Mount Vernon. The fact that his recipe for small beer discusses 30 gallon quantities indicates that he was brewing for more than just his own personal use. "Small beer" was a term widely used in the eighteenth and nineteenth centuries that described a low-alcohol ale that was typically brewed at home and consumed relatively soon after it was brewed. Presumably, if left to ferment longer, it would mature into what would have been described in the terminology of the era as "table beer" or "strong beer."

Meanwhile, the personal papers and correspondence of Thomas Jefferson, like those of George Washington, contain many references to beer and brewing. Both men made note of buying beer, and both favored Philadelphia brewers. For Jefferson, it was a man named Henry Pepper, who had immigrated from Germany as Heinrich Pfeiffer and had anglicized his name. During the 1790s, Jefferson was a regular patron of Pepper's brewery on Fifth Street.

While George Washington's interest in the brewer's art preceded the Revolutionary War and his presidency, Jefferson's appears to have come later in life. Whereas George Washington favored porter and brewed small ale for his household use, the more inquisitive Jefferson was more eclectic when it came to beer-making. In addition to his experimenting with corn, rather than barley, as a fermentable starch in some of his beer, we know from his letters that he also brewed wheat beer at his estate at Monticello.

Shortly after he left office, Jefferson happened to cross paths with a man named Joseph Coppinger, one of the most interesting characters in the early brewing history of the United States. Coppinger was a self-styled "Porter Brewer from Europe," who had first drifted onto the American brewing scene at Pittsburgh in about 1802. For about a year, he was a partner, along with Peter Shiras, in Pittsburgh's Point Brewery. Then he pulled out inexplicably and moved to New York.

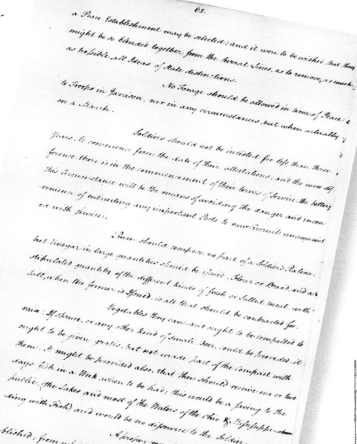

Left: General George Washington was a constant champion of a beer ration for his troops. In his letter to Alexander Hamilton of May 2, 1783, he wrote that "If spruce, or any other kind of small Beer, could be provided, it ought to be given gratis, but not made part of the Compact with [the troops]." (*Library of Congress*) *Below*: General Washington bids farewell to his commanders after the war. (*Collection of the author*)

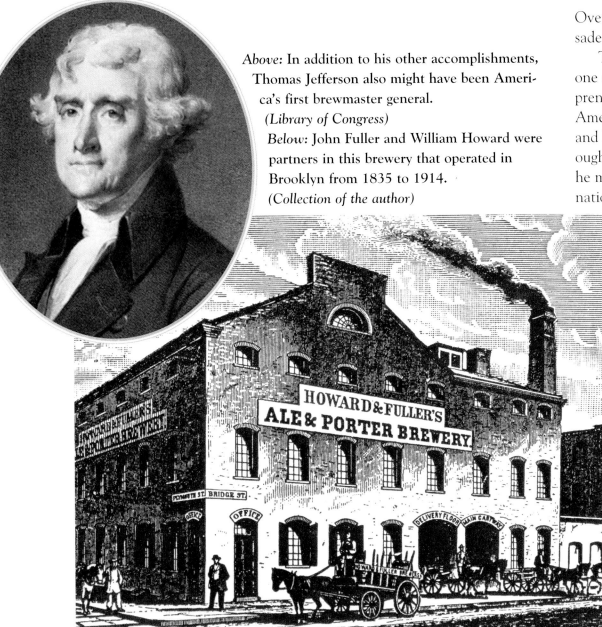

Above: In addition to his other accomplishments, Thomas Jefferson also might have been America's first brewmaster general.
(Library of Congress)
Below: John Fuller and William Howard were partners in this brewery that operated in Brooklyn from 1835 to 1914.
(Collection of the author)

Over the next few years his peculiar crusade began to take shape.

The Porter Brewer from Europe was one of those energetic dreamers and entrepreneurs who would help make shape America's future. Coppinger had a dream, and his dream was that the United States ought to have a National Brewery. By this he meant not simply a brewery that was national in the way that Adolphus Busch would later dream of a national brewery, but a national brewery in the same sense that the new nation had an Army, a Navy, a Post Office and a Supreme Court. On December 16, 1810, Coppinger sat down at his desk and outlined his plan in a personal letter to President James Madison which is still preserved in the Library of Congress:

"I am not fortunate enough to have it in my power to interest wealthy and influential characters in the request I am about to make to you. Still I am not without hopes of ultimate success in calling your attention to what I have long had earnestly at heart, that is the establishment of a Brewing Company at Washington as a national object. It has in my view the greatest importance as it would unquestionably tend to improve the quality of our Malt Liquors in every part of the Union and serve to counteract the baneful influence of ardent spirits on the health and morals of our fellow citizens."

Coppinger went on to remind Madison of the profitability of the major breweries in the United Kingdom, which then included both Bass and Guinness. Coppinger suggested that the United States National Brewery could be built and put into operation for $20,000, a sum to be raised by the sale of what amounted to brewery bonds of $500 and $1,000 denominations. He went on to promised Madison a 200 percent profit on the sale of ale and porter in bottles.

Not waiting for a reply, Coppinger wrote another letter to the President five days later in which he underscored the notion that "those families who are in the custom of using malt liquor freely as their common drink all summer, keep and preserve their health while their less fortunate neighbors who are deprived of it are the victims of fever and disease."

Madison passed Coppinger's communiques on to former President Jefferson for his comments. Jefferson considered the matter, but before anything substantial could be undertaken, the United States found itself embroiled in the chaos of the War of 1812.

In 1815, as the war drew to a close, Coppinger published his book, *The American Brewer & Maltster's Assistant*, which included a section on brewing beer with Indian corn. This book is known to have caught Jefferson's fancy, and letters preserved in the Library of Congress clearly show that the former president was writing to bookstores inquiring about Coppinger's book even before it was published. It is not known whether Coppinger — or Jefferson for that matter — had any direct contact with any Indian brewers.

After he finished his book, Coppinger once again turned to his National Brewery idea. On April 6, 1815, he again raised the idea with Jefferson, hoping to enlist the support of the elder statesman. On April 25, Jefferson responded that "I have no doubt, either in a moral or economical view, of the desirableness to introduce a taste for malt liquors instead of that for ardent spirits. . . . The business of brewing is now so much introduced in every state, that it appears to me to need no other encouragement than to increase the number of customers. I do not think it a case where a company need form itself merely on patriotic principles, because there is a sufficiency of private capital which would embark itself in the business if there were a demand."

At this point, Jefferson begged off. The third president went on to say that he considered himself "too old and too fond of quiet" to get involved in the scheme. He mentioned to Coppinger — brewer to brewer — that he was now brewing wheat beer at Monticello, and he closed in wishing the Porter Brewer from Europe a hearty "best wishes."

Above: Enjoying mugs of ale in an early American tavern. One can almost imagine George Washington or Thomas Jefferson stepping in from the chilly outdoors to have a couple. (*Collection of the author*)

Above left: **Matthew Vassar is remembered for founding Vassar College in 1861, and also for his long career as a brewer. In 1810, at the age of 18, he took over his family's small brewery in Poughkeepsie, New York and built it into one of the country's largest.**
(*Collection of the author*)
Above: **Miller's Tavern in New York's Hudson River Valley was a brewpub frequented by New York governor and later president, Martin Van Buren.**
(*Library of Congress*)

While Jefferson had confirmed it as a good idea, he had decided that realistically, there was no reason for the government to get involved when there were enough commercial breweries sprouting up in the land — and for Coppinger not to bother him any more.

One can only imagine what might have happened if Jefferson had actually taken an interest. What if Jefferson had supported and championed the idea? Could Thomas Jefferson have come back into the government as our first Brewmaster General? We have Alexander Hamilton, the first Secretary of the Treasury, pictured on the $10-bill. Imagine Thomas Jefferson pictured on 11-ounce, government-issue bottles.

Even though Washington and Jefferson, as well as many of their peers, probably brewed significant quantities of beer in their day, both were merely gentleman brewers. They were in it for the beer and not to create an economically viable ven-

ture. Another important name in early American history *was*, coincidentally a commercial brewer.

This was Matthew Vassar, best known today for having endowed the college in Poughkeepsie, New York that bears his name. Matthew's father, James Vassar, was a home-brewer who went commercial around 1801. His customer base included wagon stops along the Hudson River from Poughkeepsie to New York City. The business flourished, and in 1810, Matthew and his brother took over the business.

When the original brewery burned a year later, young Matthew — just a lad of 19 — established a brewpub and tavern in the basement of a courthouse. In business, they say that the three most important things are location, location and location. Vassar's choice of a location would certainly have been good for rebuilding a business. In 1813, Matthew Vassar rebuilt the family brewery at Poughkeepsie, and added a second brewing plant in 1832. Matthew Vassar himself was active in the business until after the Civil War, by which time he was brewing 30,000 barrels of beer annually.

Looking at archetypes in the early chapters of American history, we see Joseph Coppinger as the archetypical dreamer of big ideas and Matthew Vassar was the model of a successful early nineteenth century entrepreneur. In addition to his brewing operations, he acquired farmland as far away at Wisconsin in order to control his own supply of hops. After his retirement, his company continued to produce beer until 1895.

The Vassar Brewery may have been one of the largest of the great English-style ale breweries in America at the beginning of the nineteenth century, but its longevity is far and away eclipsed by that on a contemporary upstart in rural Pennsylvania. In 1829, David G. Yuengling, a brewer from the German state of Wurttemberg, arrived in the Schuylkill County village of Pottsville. Here in the Appalachian foothills, Yuengling established what he called — with a nod to a familiar patriotic symbol — the Eagle Brewery. Whereas Vassar's brewery was a fading memory at the dawn of the twentieth century, Yuengling's brewery would still be going strong in the twenty-first century. When Yuengling's second son, Frederick, took over in 1873, the company was renamed as D.G. Yuengling & Son. Under this name, it survives to this day — still under family ownership — as the oldest brewery in the United States.

In 1829, when David Yuengling started his business, one of his staple products was, naturally, porter. This beverage would gradually fade into obscurity in the twentieth century, leaving the Yuengling brewery as perhaps the only porter brewer in the United States in the decades prior to the craft brewery revolution of the 1980s.

As David Yuengling was stirring his first batch of wort in Pottsville, the brewing industry in the United States had matured and there was a general decline in per capita beer consumption in America. However, as students of economic cycles know, everything is on pendulum. The decline of the industry in the 1820s and 1830s only set the stage for an event of truly enormous proportions. This would be an entirely new beer style, and an entirely different brewing method.

From its English colonial roots, the role of beer and brewing in American life and in the American economy would change dramatically in the middle quarters of the nineteenth century.

Above: George Hitchner's Alloway Tavern in the New Jersey town of the same name, operated as a brewpub between 1820 and 1826. When this photo was taken in 1937, you could still buy draft beer here, but it was probably not brewed on the premises. (*Library of Congress*)

Chapter 2

THE LAGER BREWERS ARRIVE

HE BEER STYLE THAT WOULD ALTER the course of American brewing history, and define it for nearly 140 years, arrived on the scene in about 1840 as part of the first sizable wave of immigrants from Germany. Lager was invented in the mountains of Central Europe, roughly in the region that now comprises now Austria, the German state of Bavaria and the Czech state of Bohemia.

Gabriel Sedlmayr of the Spaten Brewery in Munich is credited with having perfected and defined lager as a style in the 1830s, and it was first brewed commercially in 1840 by Spaten and by the Schwechat Brewery in Vienna, both of which are still in business in the twenty-

first century. Two years later, brewers in Pilsen in Bohemia started brewing a lighter lager that they dubbed "Pilsner" in order to distinguish it from the more amber Munich and Vienna lagers. Today, the original Pilsner brewery in Pilsen still markets their lager worldwide under the brand name "Pilsner Urquell," meaning "the original Pilsner."

The German word lager means "to store." The yeast used for lager differs from that used in ale and stout. The latter are fermented with top-fermenting *Saccharomyces cerevisiae* yeast at cellar temperatures, while lager is fermented for a much longer period using bottom-fermenting yeast at temperatures that dip near freezing. Though bottom-fermenting yeast strains were used throughout the nineteenth century, it was Emil Christian Hansen, working at the Carlsberg Brewery in Copenhagen, who in 1883, isolated the *Saccharomyces carlsbergensis* yeast strain that has been widely used in lager brewing since that time.

During the 1840s, a social and economic upheaval in Europe, especially in the patchwork of German-speaking principalities, turned the trickle of German immigration to America into a flood. Awaiting the immigrants were not only a handful of lager brewers, but profitable business opportunities for would-be lager brewers. For the next century, German immigrants and their families would dominate 90 percent of the brewing industry in the United States.

It is widely believed that lager yeast first arrived in the United States in 1840 in the possession of a man named Johann Wagner. A brewmaster from Bavaria, Wagner immigrated to Philadelphia and set up a small brewery on Poplar Street. Over the next several years, lager brewing gradually gained a foothold in the city. Wagner shared his yeast with his friend George Manger, who started a brewery on Second Street. Next came Charles (Karl) Wolf,

Manger's former employer. A German brewer, Wolf had started a sugar refinery in Philadelphia, but when he got his hands on lager yeast, he promptly returned to his former profession. As Wolf was opening his brewery on Dillwyn Street in 1844, lager brewing had spread from Philadelphia to cities such as New York and Cincinnati, where there were sizable German communities.

Everywhere that the German immigrants congregated, a lager brewery was

Right: **Enjoying a dark lager.** *(Collection of the author)*
Below: **An 1879 lager poster.** *(Library of Congress)*
Opposite: **Lager is part of the and fun at the Otzwick family picnic.** *(Collection of the author)*

soon established. In Cincinnati, for example, the first lager brewer is said to have been Franz Fortmann, who took over the Agneil & Fleishman Bavarian Brewery in 1844. In New York, which had alternated with Philadelphia as the brewing capital of the United States since before there was a United States, lager breweries and German biergartens proliferated. The first may have belonged to George Gillig, although he had some early competition from Frederick and Maximilian Schaefer, whose name would be a household word among New York beer lovers for more than a century.

In Baltimore, where English-style breweries had existed for a century, George Rossmarck began brewing lager in 1846. He was soon followed by Frederick Ludwig in 1848 and by George Rost in 1849. One of the city's most interesting lager brewers — especially for the architectural legacy he left to Baltimore — was Johann "John" Frederick Weissner. He was a late-comer to the lager revolution, arriving during the Civil War, but he bequeathed the city an architectural landmark that is clearly a symbol of the lager revolution. Weissner began brewing in 1863 on North Gay Street, but he is best remembered for the grand German-Ameri-

can brewery building he built on the same site in 1887. The flamboyant architecture made it what architectural historians once called one of the finest examples of the "Teutonic Brewery" style in the United States. It was certainly a landmark in northeast Baltimore, where it was referred to as the "Germanic Pagoda." After Weissner himself passed away in 1897, the company also remained a Baltimore landmark. It would emerge from Prohibition as American Brewing and continued in operation until 1973.

Lager had reached American shores at an auspicious time. By the 1820s, the per capita consumption of English beer styles in the United States had begun to wane. In the 1820s and 1830s, new beverages had crept onto American tables in expanding quantities. French wine, always popular on the tables of the gentry, was more widely available than ever, as was Caribbean rum. Meanwhile, whiskey was becoming increasingly popular. The Whiskey Rebellion of 1794 had been about taxation, with the people living west of the Appalachians insisting that they not be taken advantage of by the more populous East. The fact that whiskey was the centerpiece of the rebellion only goes to show how important the small distillers in the West had now become to the national economy. By the late 1820s, the "West" was emerging as an important part of the United States, not merely an incidental anteroom to the long established coastal civilization. The election in 1828 of the first Western President of the United States — Andrew "Old Hickory" Jackson of Tennessee — was one indication of the cultural shift. The rise of corn whisky from Tennessee and Kentucky was another. Westerners had discovered that the abundant surplus of corn was much more useful in distilling than in brewing.

With the lager revolution, the decline in beer consumption was, at last reversed. Of course, it was not only Germans who found themselves enjoying a glass of lager. The drinking of the golden brew also soon expanded beyond the German immigrant enclaves to the rest of the population. Descendants of English colonists, who had eschewed their grandfathers' porter in favor of whiskey and rum, quickly developed a taste for the cold beverage from Bavaria.

Americans now insisted that lager was not actually an intoxicating beverage — which of course was not actually true. A nineteenth century article in *Harper's Monthly* recalls that "During a famous trial some years since, soon after lager found its way to America, evidence was introduced to show that the beverage was not intoxicating. Old-time imbibers one after another testified as to capacity of stomach and steadiness of head, until the climax was reached in a worthy descendant of old King Cole, who claimed an ability to dispose of 60 glasses at a single sitting. The advocates of total abstinence stood aghast at the disclosure, while even the moderate drinkers retreated in disorder."

Despite the rise of lagers, ale brewing survived. Throughout the nineteenth century, it was not unusual to see tavern signs that advertised it along with lager. In Chicago, when Johann "John" Huck and Johann "John" Schneider arrived in 1847 to set up their lager business, they had stiff competition from the Lill & Diversey ale brewery. Founded by William Lill in 1833, this business has been described as being the largest brewery in the West in the decades leading up to the Civil War. Indeed, records show that Lill and his partner, Michael Diversey, exported their ale and porter northwest as far as St. Paul, northeast to Buffalo and down the Mississippi as far as New Orleans. Until the eve of the Civil War, when exports to the South ended abruptly, the output of the

It must be springtime, for this German American maid is romping with a goat, the symbol of bock beer, brewed for the spring. (*Library of Congress*)

Below: Popular with German-Americans, bock beer originated in Einbeck in Lower Saxony. The goat is the symbol because "bock" in German is billy goat. In the local dialect, Einbeck is pronounced like "Einbock," which sounds like "ein Bock," meaning "a goat." (*Library of Congress*)

Lill & Diversey enterprise was nearly 45,000 barrels annually.

Wherever German immigrants landed during this era, lager breweries would spring up. Germans immigrants also arrived in Texas at about this time, and San Antonio was rapidly becoming a major center of German-American culture. Wilhelm — later William — Menger became the first commercial lager brewer in the Lone Star State when he started his Western Brewery on Blum Street in San Antonio in 1855. After the Civil War, San Antonio would emerge as the brewing capital of the former Confederacy. In Cincinnati, the first lager brewer is said to have been Franz Fortmann, who took over at Agneil & Fleishman's Bavarian Brewery in 1844.

In the headwaters of the Mississippi, were the Twin Cities of what was to become the state of Minnesota in 1858. What was probably the first brewery in the future state capital of St. Paul was started by Anton Yoerg in 1848 on South Washington Street. Through 1855, Yoerg's establishment was joined on the roster of breweries by the City Brewery, the North Star Brewery, the North Mississippi Brewery, and the Fleckenstein Brothers Brewery. In 1860, Andrew Keller opened his Pittsburgh Brewery in St. Paul. Before the Civil War was over, it would be owned by a man named Theodore Hamm.

St. Paul's "Twin City," Minneapolis, saw the founding of two major brewing operations during the 1850s. Gottlieb Gluek founded a company under his own name, while Johann "John" Orth started what was to become Minneapolis Brewing & Malting, better known by the brand name of its flagship lager — Grain Belt.

Out west, on the distant Pacific shore, Oregon Territory (then containing both the modern states of Oregon and Washington) was not added as a territory until 1846. California had briefly declared itself a republic in 1846 with the aid of United States forces, and Mexico formally ceded the territory to the United States in 1848. California would become a state in 1850, and Oregon would follow in 1859. By this time, both states had a thoroughly evolved brewing history.

The Golden West's largest state, California earned it's nickname, "the Golden State" for the 1849 Gold Rush. The precious yellow metal was discovered in phenomenal abundance in the Sierra Nevada foothills in 1848, and when news of this reached the East, it touched off what has been characterized as the biggest voluntary mass migration in human history. San Francisco, a sleepy outpost on a perfect natural harbor, blossomed into a magnificent metropolis in less than two years. At the same time, the city of the Golden Gate became the most important brewing city west of the cities bordering the Mississippi River. It has been said that until the Civil War, half of all the United States breweries west of the Father of Waters were in San Francisco.

When he penned the definitive history of California's early days, Hubert Howe Bancroft noted that in 1837, a San Franciscan named William "Billy the Brewer" McGlove became the first Euro-American to have brewed beer west of the Mississippi. This would place San Francisco ahead of Milwaukee among America's great brewing cities. Other data indicates that

Left: An 1857 poster from Boston. *Above:* An old drinking song celebrates lager. (*Library of Congress*)

bottled beer was being imported into San Francisco by 1843 and that ale and porter were abundantly available there by the Gold Rush year of 1849.

By the time of the Gold Rush, San Francisco had many breweries. It has been said that half of the breweries west of the cities along the Mississippi River were located here. This may be an exaggeration, but it is nevertheless a good story, and one rooted in fact. William Bull's Empire Brewery at Market and Second Streets is the earliest one mentioned in a city directory. Adam Schuppert's California Brewery is also noted in other sources as having been extant in 1849. Though many breweries probably came and went during these turbulent times, there were at least 15 in San Francisco by 1856. These included Schuppert's, as well as Jacob Gundlach's Bavarian Brewery, Jacob Specht's San Francisco Brewery and the Seidenstrecker & Rathe Washington Brewery. Both the Eagle and Eureka breweries were specifically listed as brewing ale and porter.

Lager brewing presented problems in San Francisco, however. As the Gold Rush was sweeping California, the lager revolution was sweeping the rest of the nation. It was only natural that the thirsty "Forty-Niners" would want a pint of lager. How-

ever, lager fermentation requires more than just lager yeast. It requires temperatures that are very near freezing. Like lager's native Bavaria, cities such as New York, Philadelphia and Milwaukee take freezing temperatures for granted and enough ice can be harvested in the winter to be stored all year long.

San Francisco's temperatures in the bitter cold months of June and July can appear to dip below 32 degrees with the wind chill factor, but it almost never actually freezes. In the 1850s, ice had to be imported from Alaska or brought down from the High Sierra by wagon. Both options were not economical for brewing. The solution, arrived at by an anonymous San Francisco brewer and soon adopted throughout the Golden State, was to ferment beer at warmer "ale" temperatures while using lager yeast. Because the yeast flourished as it continued to ferment at warmer than accustomed temperatures, there was a huge build-up of carbon dioxide and a large blast of foam and carbon dioxide when kegs were tapped. Probably for this reason, the hybrid beer style apparently came to be called "steam beer," although no one can say with certainty why the word "steam" came to be associated with beer. Since early in the twentieth century, Anchor Brewing Company of San Francisco alone has used this quaint name for its unique beer, and "Steam" has become a trademark of Anchor Brewing for its Anchor Steam Beer. Though the Anchor name would not be assigned to the brewery until 1896, Anchor's roots can be traced to the company started by German immigrant brewer Gottlieb Brekle, who had arrived in San Francisco with his family prior to 1854, the date that he applied for citizenship. The little brewery he established on Pacific Avenue between Larkin and Hyde Streets would one day become known as Anchor.

As the Gold Rush brought tens of thousands to the canyons and placers of the Sierras, enterprising brewers naturally followed. In the Sierra Nevada gold mining towns, breweries are known to have existed in places such as Placerville and Downieville in the 1850s. Christopher Kuhn is said to have established the first "lager" brewery in Los Angeles in 1854,

but he probably was producing a product more like that which the San Franciscans referred to as steam beer. The City of Angels was at as much of a loss for ice as was San Francisco.

Up the coast in the Pacific Northwest, the evolution of commercial brewing followed that of California — but not by much. In Oregon Territory, the new city of Portland — originally "Stumptown" — soon emerged as the brewing center of the Northwest. Coincidentally, it would take on a similar role 130 years later during the craft brewing revolution. The first brewery in Portland is believed to have been the City Brewery, established by Henry Saxer in 1852 and operated by him for exactly ten years. In 1862, he would sell out to Henry Weinhard, a man whose name would be closely associated with Oregon brewing for more than a century. Weinhard had come to Portland from just across the Columbia River in Vancouver, Washington. Here, in 1859, he had taken over

Opposite Advertising New York's Feigenspan Brewery. *Above:* The Union in Virginia City, Nevada supplied thirsty miners beginning in 1866. *(Library of Congress)* *Inset:* Henry Weinhard. *(Bill Yenne illustration)*

the brewery started by Johann "John" Muench in 1856, Washington's first commercial brewery.

In the Rockies, Colorado's first brewery, the Rocky Mountain Brewery, was opened in Denver in 1859, a year after the Colorado Gold Rush began. As elsewhere during this era, the proprietors were German: Charles (Karl) Tascher and F. Z. Solomon.

Of all the cities in America where German immigrants settled and founded breweries, one would rise to so dominate the industry that for a century, that its very name would be as synonymous with brewing — just as that of Detroit would later be of the automobile industry. Milwaukee, Wisconsin was a young city when the Lager revolution came to American shores. It was formed in 1838 through the consolidation of several fur trading settlements, although it was not officially incorporated as a city until 1846.

Milwaukee's fame would be tied to a short list of great brewing companies, which were in turn, tied to a short list of great brewing families. The great dynasties who made the beers that "made Milwaukee famous" included those of the Best brothers, Frederick Miller, Captain Frederick Pabst, Valentin Blatz and Joseph Schlitz. Indeed, it was the Schlitz company that coined the advertising slogan describing its product as "The Beer That Made Milwaukee Famous." The implication was already there — Milwaukee *was* famous, and that was *because* of beer.

Left: Milwaukee brewing patriarch Philip Best. *(Bill Yenne illustration) Below:* This 1898 poster for the play *Hogan's Alley* depicts family fun and joyous chaos in the typical American beer hall. *(Library of Congress)*

Three breweries were established in Milwaukee in 1840, coincidentally the same year that Johann Wagner first brought lager yeast to America. The first of these was, however, an ale and porter brewery. Known as the Milwaukee Brewery, this establishment was started on Huron Street by a partnership of three Welshmen, John Davis, Richard Owens and William Pawlett. The trio brewed not only ale and porter, but they also distilled whiskey. According to the city's official history, the men started brewing with a five-barrel capacity, but imported a 40-barrel copper brew kettle from Chicago in 1844.

Milwaukee's first lager brewer was probably Herman Reuthlisberger (aka Riedelschoefer) in 1840. He named his new facility on Virginia Street the German Brewery, apparently to underscore the fact that he was brewing lager and the Milwaukee was *not*. A year later, Riedelschoefer sold his business to J.R. Maier, who renamed it as the Lake Brewery. Maier, in turn, sold out to Franz Neukirch in 1844. In 1848, Neukirch took on a partner, C.J. Melms, whose family would continue to run the business as the Menominee Brewery until 1869.

Finally, the third of the class of 1840, was the brewery of Stotz & Krill on Ogden Street. The following years saw several new breweries come into existence. In 1841, the Eagle Brewery opened on Prairie Street, and in 1843, William Pawlett, late of the Milwaukee Brewery bought into this business. In 1842, the Munzinger & Koethe Brewery opened on Burrell Street, rounding out the first generation of Milwaukee breweries.

Three years later, David Gipfel constructed his first lager brewery in Milwaukee. Six years later, ownership passed to Karl Wilhelm (Charles) Gipfel, possibly David's son. Charles operated the company under the name Union Brewery and in 1853, he built a brewery building on Chestnut Street (later Juneau Avenue) that would be recognized a century later as

Inset: Jacob Best. (*Bill Yenne illustration*) *Above:* Cold, dark lager. (*Library of Congress*)

Left: **Milwaukee brewing legend Frederick Miller.**
(Bill Yenne illustration) Below: **Miller's original Plank Road Brewery in Wauwatosa, Wisconsin.**
(Courtesy of the brewery)

the oldest surviving brewhouse in the state of Wisconsin. Herman Schliebitz, who operated the company between 1892 and 1894 as the Weiss Beer Brewery was the last brewer on the site.

The first of the legendary Milwaukee brewing families arrived on the scene in 1844 in the person of Jacob Best, who opened his Empire Brewery on Chestnut Street. His sons, especially Charles and Phillip, would go on to be the men who helped "make Milwaukee famous." Charles would start the company that evolved into Miller Brewing, while Phillip's daughter, Maria, married a steamship captain named Frederick Pabst. Phillip, originally in partnership with brother Jacob, Jr., stayed on to take over the family business in 1853, but Charles struck out on his own.

The Menomenee Valley Brewery was established by Charles Best in 1850 at Wauwatosa, near Milwaukee. He called it the Plank Road Brewery, because of practice of paving the streets in timber-rich Wisconsin with wood. He ran it for only a couple of years, but it reopened in 1854 under the proprietorship of a young German immigrant who anglicized his name as Frederick Edward John Miller. The brewery's name was promptly changed to Miller Brewing, although the company would briefly revive the "Plank Road

Brewery" name for specialty products at the end of the twentieth century.

Frederick Miller was born in 1824, into an influential family from Riedlingen in the southern German state of Wurttemberg, the same state to which the Yuengling brewing family in Pennsylvania traces its lineage. From the age of 14, however, he lived in France, and he apprenticed at a brewery owned by his uncle in the Lorraine city of Nancy. He later recrossed the Rhine to take over operations at the Royal Hohenzollern brewery in Sigmaringen. In 1854, Miller and his wife Josephine came to the United States with a sizable nest egg that is mentioned in some accounts to have been a gift from the Hohenzollern family. After living briefly in New York City, the Millers and their young son Joseph relocated to Milwaukee, where Frederick acquired the Plank Road Brewery. Company records indicate that he brewed his first batch of beer in 1855, and a newspaper account noted that he had also

opened a beer hall on East Water Street in Milwaukee in 1857.

In 1860, when Philip Best became the sole owner his father's Empire Brewery, the company became the Philip Best Company. By this time, Philip's daughters had each married a young man with an interest in the brewing industry — Emil Schandien and Captain Frederick Pabst. The captain earned his rank running merchant vessels on the Great Lakes. Philip Best retired in 1864, placing his sons-in-law in charge of the company that he'd inherited from his father. By now, the corporate family tree that began two decades earlier with Jacob Best, Sr. included three of the principal names in Milwaukee brewing history — Best, Miller and Pabst. Schandien would soon be eclipsed by his ambitious brother-in-law. With Captain Pabst's hand at the throttle, the Philip Best Company had become the largest brewery in Milwaukee by the 1870s.

Inset: Milwaukee brewing pioneer Valentin Blatz. (*Bill Yenne illustration*) *Above:* An advertising poster for Blatz Milwaukee Lager. (*Library of Congress*)

Womanly

A sweet woman, the picture of health, speaking with enthusiasm, said, "I don't see why you do not send out women to talk to women about the merits of Pabst Malt Extract, The "Best" Tonic. There are so many women that are run down, with nerves shattered and a lack of vitality, feeling a sort of restless indecision which is an outgrowth of overexertion, that if you could get a woman who knows as thoroughly as I do how "Best" Tonic will build one up, and who has enough earnestness to tell them about it, you would certainly have a largely increased sale. There was Mrs.—, who was thin as she could be, and her poor little baby puny and undeveloped. I told her about "Best" Tonic. In three weeks you ought to see the difference. Why, the improvement is something great; even the baby feels it and shows it. I tell you the women of this country ought to know about this, and I am going to do my part to tell them."

Pabst Malt Extract, The "Best" Tonic.

ASK FOR "PABST"

PERFECTION IN BREWING IS REACHED IN AMERICA

Left: Pabst takes credit (sort of) for getting the Forty-Niners to the Golden West. *Below:* The Pabst Brewery in Milwaukee. (*Collection of the author*) Opposite: A classic American brewery painting. (*Library of Congress*)

Pabst Brewery. Milwaukee, Wis.

Across the state of Wisconsin in LaCrosse, John Gund and Gottlieb Heileman founded their small City Brewery on South Third Street in 1858. Gund, who had previously owned another company in LaCrosse, left Heileman and went independent again. Gottlieb Heileman continued to build his business, as did his family after his death in 1878. The G. Heileman Brewing Company would eventually grow to national prominence, not through the vehicle of a single national brand like Pabst or Schlitz, but through an amazing amalgam of important, formerly independent brands, including — nearly a century later — Blatz.

In Chippewa Falls, another notable small Wisconsin hometown brewing company was that founded by Jacob Leinenkugel and John Miller (no relation to Frederick Miller) in 1867. Located on top of Big Eddy Springs, the brewery was known as the Spring Brewery until 1898 and was long known for its distinctive Indian maiden head logo. The logo reflects the brewery's location in "Indian Head Country," so named because of the Indian profile created on maps by the meanderings of the Mississippi River along the Wisconsin-Minnesota border near Chippewa Falls. The brand survived though most of the twentieth century as a strong independent brand with a very devoted following. In 1987 the company was purchased by Miller Brewing.

Revitalized by the introduction of lager, the United States brewing industry enjoyed tremendous growth during the 1850s. The number of breweries grew much faster than the population. From 431 American breweries in 1850, the number nearly tripled to 1,269 in 1860, while the population increased by just a third. More than three quarters of the production was still centered in

New York and Pennsylvania, but the fastest-growing centers were in the upper Midwest, especially in Chicago and Milwaukee. During the Civil War, the brewing industry, which was primarily concentrated north of the Mason-Dixon line, found itself supporting the Union war effort in ways it had not expected. In 1861 the Internal Revenue System was established to use income taxes to finance the war, but the following year, the brewing industry was singled out — a one dollar tax was levied on each barrel of beer produced in the United States.

In response to government taxation and a growing temperance movement, 37 breweries in New York City came together in 1862 to form the industry's first trade organization, which became known as the United States Brewers' Association in 1864. This organization would grow and expand with the industry for the next half century.

During the postwar half century two major trends would be seen in the American brewing industry. First there was the evolution of the giant mega-brewers, and second was the proliferation of hometown breweries nearly everywhere in the United States.

FRANK JONES' BREWERY & MALT HOUSES.
PORTSMOUTH, N.H.
DEPOT 82 & 84 WASHINGTON ST. BOSTON.

Chapter 3

BREWING BECOMES A MAJOR AMERICAN INDUSTRY

IT WAS DURING THE HALF CENTURY THAT followed the Civil War, the years from 1865 to 1915, that the United States came of age as a major economic power in the world. In both industry and agriculture, the United States grew to international prominence as a producer and exporter, while both of these sectors contributed greatly to the growth and prosperity of the nation internally.

This was true of most industries, and the brewing industry was no exception. The number of breweries in the United States continued to mushroom. As we've noted above, that number tripled between 1850 and 1860. By 1873, it had more than tripled again — from 1,269 to 4,131. Meanwhile, the nation's population increased by only 23 percent.

Just as significant was that the volume of beer being produced had also grown. From just over a million barrels in 1860, the industry had seen an increase to 6.6 million barrels in 1870, and 9.6 million in 1873. This meant that the breweries were averaging about 800 barrels a year in 1860, and 2,332 barrels a year by 1873. Of course, there were a number of major breweries that were producing many times the average.

The largest beer market in the United States was the nation's largest metropolitan area. The five boroughs which now constitute New York City grew from 1.2 million people in 1860 to nearly two million in 1880 and 3.4 million by the turn of the century. At the center of North America's largest metropolitan area, New York saw the rise of a number of major brewing companies.

During these years, the largest brewery in New York City was also the largest brewery in the United States, and that brewery belonged to George Ehret. Trained as a brewer in Germany, Ehret had arrived in New York City in 1857 at the age of 22. Ehret is said to have gone to work for Anton Hupfel, whose brewery was located at Third Avenue and 161st Street. In 1866, Ehret struck out on his own, building his own lager brewery on 92nd Street between Second and Third Avenues in the Yorkville district of New York City. The location was auspicious, for nearby 86th Street would be the center of German-American culture in the five boroughs for the next century.

Ehret named his business the Hell Gate Brewery, after a treacherous section

Above: An American brewery wagon *(Courtesy of Carl Miller) Opposite:* **Pabst Park in Milwaukee.** *(Collection of the author)*

Below: **The Frederick and Max Schaefer Brewery in New York.** *(Collection of the author)*

Above: **Brewery king George Ehret.** *(Bill Yenne illustration). Below:* **New York-brewed Wurzburger.** *(Collection of the author)*

of the nearby East River. His brewery produced its first brew in January 1867, and within five years, it was producing nearly 34,000 barrels annually. Production topped 100,000 barrels in 1874 and exceeded 180,000 within five years, making Ehret's Hell Gate the largest brewery on the continent. The actual brewery's physical plant itself grew to encompass an entire city block, with stables and other ancillary facilities reaching as far north as 94th Street. The company surpassed 400,000 barrels in 1890 and would exceed 600,000 annually by the turn of the century.

Also among the pantheon of great names from the expansive early days of New York brewing was that of the brothers Schaefer. Frederick Schaefer arrived in New York City from Prussia in 1838, and went to work brewing beer for Sebastian Sommers's brewery on Broadway near 18th Street. A couple of years later, when lager suddenly came on the scene in Germany, there were excited ripples throughout the German-American community. At about this time, Frederick's brother, Maximilian, arrived in New York City with a sample of lager yeast. In 1842, Frederick Schaefer bought out his boss, and he and Max began brewing lager.

The brothers moved their operations to Seventh Avenue near West 16th Street in 1845, and later to Fourth Avenue (Park Avenue after 1860) and East 51st Street, just north of where the New York Central Railroad would later build Grand Central Station. Frederick died in 1897, and Max passed away in 1904, by which time, the F. & M. Schaefer Brewing Company had grown into one of New York's great brewing enterprises. Max's son and heir, Rudolf Schaefer, bought out Frederick's heirs and took sole control of the company. In 1916, after 67 years in their huge, red brick landmark brewery on Park Avenue, Rudolf Schaefer became one of the first big Manhattan brewers to move operations entirely to Brooklyn. He selected a vast tract on Kent Street overlooking the East River.

Joining the German names in the pantheon of great New York brewers was one of the last great English names in nineteenth century American brewing — Ballantine. Peter Ballantine was born in 1791, grew up in Ayr, on the shores of Scotland's

Firth of Clyde and immigrated to America in 1820. He began brewing in Albany in 1833, but moved his operation to Newark, New Jersey in 1840 in order to be closer to the rapidly growing market in New York City. Here, he joined forces with Erastus Patterson in acquiring a brewery that had been founded by General John Cumming in 1805. Peter Ballantine became the sole proprietor of the company in 1847. A decade later, the company became P. Ballantine & Sons, as the younger members of the family were incorporated into the management of the firm.

While nearly everyone else had turned to lager, Ballantine's was also one of the last great names in nineteenth century ale brewing. It is probably not an exaggeration to say that P. Ballantine & Sons was, at its peak, the largest ale brewery that existed in the United States during the nineteenth century.

By 1879, the company was the second largest brewing operation the New York metropolitan area — and the sixth largest nationally — with an annual output of more than 100,000 barrels. Meanwhile, Peter Ballantine inaugurated his legendary trademark. As the story is told, Ballantine had observed three rings left on a table by a wet beer glass. In those three rings of

beer, Ballantine saw a graphically pleasing logo. He decided that these three interlocking rings stood for the three principles that were most important to him in his product. He named the three rings "purity,

Above: **A nineteenth century New York street scene. Ruppert Beer, depicted here, would not actually arrive on the scene for a generation.** *(Courtesy of Joe Radman)*

Left: A label for Haberle's Congress Beer from Syracuse. *(Collection of the author) Below:* A teamster making his rounds, delivering his goods. *(Courtesy of Carl Miller) Opposite:* This Kenosha, Wisconsin street scene includes a Miller Brewing Company tied house. *(Courtesy of the brewery)*

strength, and flavor." Beginning in 1879, the three-ring logo would appear on Ballantine packaging and advertising for more than a century.

In that same year, the company acquired a second brewery in Newark from the Schalk Brothers, who had begun brewing in 1852. Members of the Schalk family,

meanwhile, would remain active in the brewing business around Newark until the early twentieth century. In the 1890s, Ballantine reached an annual output of half a million barrels.

Yet another New York brewing company of note — especially for what it would become in the twentieth century — was that of Samuel Liebmann. Unlike many other family businesses founded by immigrants, Liebmann's was one where the patriarch was preceded into the American brewing scene by his three sons. Joseph, Charles and Henry came to New York City from Bavaria in about 1850, and they sent for their father soon after. Known as S. Liebmann's Sons, the family brewery was in operation in 1854 on Meserole Street in the Williamsburg section of Brooklyn. It was in 1855, that the Liebmanns relocated their operation to the corner of Forrest and Bremen Streets in Bushwick. The area was then part of Long Island City, but it was later was incorporated into Brooklyn, which became a borough of New York City in 1898.

Meanwhile, Samuel Liebmann's daughters married two beer brewing brothers named Obermeyer. In 1868, David Obermeyer, along with brother-in-law Joseph Liebmann, opened shop nearby at Bremen and Noll Streets, starting the Obermeyer & Liebmann Havana Brewery. The Obermeyer & Liebmann company would operate independently from the other branch of the family business until they merged after a generation later. In a unique cooperative arrangement, the three sons would rotate the office of chief executive at S. Liebmann's Sons among themselves until after the turn of the century. A leader in technical innovation, the Liebmanns were among the first brewers in Brooklyn to install a mechanical refrigeration system. Introduced in 1870, their unit was of the type designed by the French inventor Ferdinand Carre, which used liquid ammonia compression.

Being situated in the center of a metropolitan area with more people than lived in most states, New York brewing giants like Ballantine, Ehret and Schaefer never needed to give much thought to markets

Above: Cross-town rivals Captain Frederick Pabst and Joseph Schlitz. In fact, both men helped to make Milwaukee famous. *(Bill Yenne illustrations.) Below:* Born of fire, the Schlitz slogan. *(Collection of the author)*

beyond their core market. A brewery in Manhattan or Brooklyn or Newark had more customers within a half day's drive of a brewery wagon than lived in Milwaukee, St. Louis and Chicago combined. In 1880, while New York approached two million people, Chicago had a population of just half a million, St. Louis a third of a million, and Milwaukee boasted just 115,587 people. New York brewers had no reason to think outside the box of their core market, but brewers in places such as Milwaukee and St. Louis did.

Technology would make this possible. Hand in hand with the growth of American industry in the second half of the nineteenth century was the growth of the American transportation network. In 1850, there were 9,021 miles of railroads in the United States, but the mileage tripled to 30,635 in 1860, and increased to 52,914 in 1870, even as the output of the American brewing industry grew nine-fold in the 1860s. Meanwhile, the long-anticipated transcontinental railroad — built and operated jointly by the Central Pacific and the Union Pacific — would link California to the rest of the nation in 1869.

Milwaukee became America's great brewing center by exporting beyond Wisconsin. Being from a lightly populated state — with fewer people than New York's borough of Manhattan — the Milwaukee brewers had learned the importance of wider distribution. They also benefited from the tragedy of the Great Chicago Fire of 1871, which destroyed or crippled many Chicago breweries. In the aftermath, the Windy City's thirsty citizens turned to the products of nearby Milwaukee.

By the 1870s, Captain Frederick Pabst had turned his father-in-law's business, the Philip Best Company, into the largest brewery in Milwaukee. Indeed, by then it was second only to George Ehret's huge New York City company nationally. In 1889, he took sole control of the company, renaming it Pabst Brewing. Four years later, Pabst Brewing, now America's largest, became the first brewery in United States history to exceed a million barrels of production annually.

The captain cast his distribution network far and wide, from the farms and cities of the upper Midwest to the sparsely populated Plains and Mountain West. In 1899, he audaciously began exporting into New York City, where the local brewers had a volume unmatched nearly anywhere but Milwaukee. He even opened a Pabst Hotel in New York. The captain certainly had a flair for the dramatic. In 1882, Pabst began tying blue silk ribbons around bottles of Pabst Select Beer, thus identifying the product in the minds of consumers as a first place winner. In fact, it was a prize winner, having brought home medals from the International Exposition in Paris in 1878 and at the Chicago World's Fair in 1893. The phrase "Blue Ribbon" was finally placed on Pabst bottles two years later, where it would remain through the turns of two centuries. In 1898, Pabst Select Beer was officially renamed as Pabst Blue Ribbon Beer.

When Frederick Pabst passed away on New Year's Day in 1904, Pabst Brewing was at the peak of its power. It was still the largest in the nation and Pabst Blue Ribbon was a household word from Chicago to New York City.

On the other limb of the Jacob Best, Sr. corporate family tree was Fred Miller, whose company remained an important factor and one of the important brewers in Milwaukee for the next century. From tenth place nationally and third in Milwaukee, Miller would finally emerge in the late 1970s as the second largest brewing company in the United States after Anheuser-Busch.

Pabst's biggest rival in Milwaukee during the nineteenth century, and well into the twentieth century, would be the brewery of Joseph Schlitz. The company emerged as a major player in the wake of the Great Chicago Fire of 1871. Schlitz led the effort to get emergency supplies of beer into the decimated city. Though other Milwaukee brewers became involved in this essential relief effort, the people Chicago saw and remembered the Schlitz brand name. It was a charitable act that turned into a public relations coup. Schlitz became "The Beer That Made Milwaukee Famous."

It was the Great Fire that made Schlitz famous, while Schlitz, in turn, had made Milwaukee and its brewing industry famous. The Chicago brewing industry would never fully recover its former glory, and Milwaukee became the capital of American brewing. Within a few years, Schlitz had emerged from the

Above: **The sprawling Schlitz Brewing Company campus in Milwaukee during its nineteenth century heyday.** *(Collection of the author)*

Right: A contented consumer consumes a bottle of the beer that made Milwaukee famous. *(Library of Congress)*
Below: Milwaukee was so tied to quality in beer that Emil Raddant's brewery in Shawano styled itself as a "Milwaukee" brewery. *(Collection of the author)*
Opposite: A flotilla of brewery wagons muster in the yard at the Schlitz Brewery. *(Courtesy of Carl Miller)*

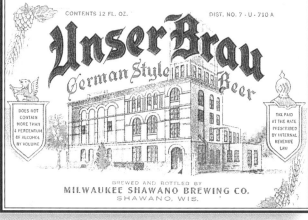

pack to become Milwaukee's number two brewer behind Captain Pabst, and the slogan survived for over a century as one of the most memorable in American brewing history. Eventually, it would surpass even Pabst.

Joseph Schlitz himself was born in Mainz in the German state of Hesse and came to Milwaukee in 1850 at the age of 20. Here, he went to work for August Krug, himself a recent German immigrant, who had started his brewery in 1849 on Chestnut Street across the street from David Gipfel's pioneer lager brewery. When Krug died in 1856, Schlitz took over management of the company. Two years later, Schlitz married Anna Krug, August's widow, and renamed the company as Joseph Schlitz Brewing. In 1874, Schlitz Brewing produced nearly 70,000 barrels, up from 50,000 barrels the year before.

Schlitz did not have long to savor the glory. In 1875, just four years after the Great Fire, he decided to make a trip back to Germany to visit relatives. He never arrived. The steamship SS *Schiller* on which he was travelling ran aground off Britain's Lands End, and Schlitz drowned. Widowed a second time, Anna would live until 1887.

Control of Joseph Schlitz Brewing now passed to August Uihlein, who had been involved with the brewery longer than Schlitz, and who had been the point man for Schlitz in organizing the effort to get the beer into Chicago after the Great Fire. Uihlein had been a Krug family friend as a child, and Schlitz had hired him as a bookkeeper in 1858 when he was just 16. In 1879, under Uihlein, Schlitz became number two in Milwaukee, producing 110,832 barrels to Pabst's 180,152 barrels. Uihlein began mass bottling of the Schlitz product in Milwaukee in 1877, and was also very aggressive in expanding the number of brewery-owned saloons, taverns and beer gardens that Schlitz operated in Milwaukee, Chicago and elsewhere. In 1893, he formally adopted the slogan "The Beer That Made Milwaukee Famous" for use in the company's advertising.

August Uihlein would manage the company for 36 years — longer than Schlitz himself — until his death in 1911. He kept Joseph Schlitz Brewing in the top five nationally.

Though he was overshadowed by Pabst and Schlitz, Valentin "Val" Blatz was a Milwaukee brewing legend who played an important part in shaping the city's mystique. His company would be Milwaukee's

Above: **The brilliant brewing entrepreneur Adolphus Busch.** *(Bill Yenne illustration) Right:* **Built in 1892, the Anheuser-Busch Brewery in St. Louis is seen here in around 1937.** *(Library of Congress)*

number three brewery for much of the latter part of the nineteenth century. Born in Germany in 1826, Blatz arrived in Milwaukee in about 1850 and started his Milwaukee brewery next door to Johann Braun's City Brewery. When Braun died in 1852, Blatz married Braun's widow and consolidated the two firms as the Val Blatz Brewery. In 1889, when a consortium of British financiers doing business as Milwaukee & Chicago Breweries Ltd., proposed a takeover and consolidation of Milwaukee's big three. Pabst and Schlitz laughed off the scheme, but Blatz parted with a share in his company.

As brewers outside of New York City moved to take advantage of marketing and transportation opportunities to export their beer beyond their core market, many important regional centers developed. In addition to Milwaukee, places such as Philadelphia, San Francisco, San Antonio and the twin cities of Minneapolis-St. Paul were important, and so too was St. Louis, Missouri.

Long before the Civil War, the first man onto the stage of commercial brewing in St. Louis was Thomas Biddle, who established his Phoenix Brewery there in about 1825. Within a generation, the Germans arrived, and the

Phoenix was taken over by the partnership of Fleischbein & Ketterer in 1835. Among the other Germans who opened breweries during the first round of German brewing in St. Louis were Wilhelm Stumpf in 1850 and George Schneider in 1852. Their respective breweries, founded on Decatur Street and Carondelet Avenue, would evolve into establishments that would play an important part in the post-Civil War generation of St. Louis brewers.

In 1857 Schneider sold his little Bavarian Brewery to Adam and Phillip Carl Hammer, who were underwritten by a loan from a wealthy St. Louis manufacturer named Eberhard Anheuser. By 1860, when the brewery once again verged on collapse, Anheuser realized he needed to take direct control of operations in order to protect his investment. The firm became known as E. Anheuser & Company's Bavarian Brewery.

Less than a year later, Anheuser's daughter Lily married a 22-year-old brewery supply salesman named Adolphus Busch. In 1864 Busch joined his father-in-law's firm and in five years, he was a partner. In 1875 the Bavarian Brewery name was dropped and the brewery became E. Anheuser and Company's

Brewing Association. In 1879, it became the Anheuser-Busch Brewing Association.

In 1880, upon the death of Eberhard Anheuser, Busch took over the company. He would soon prove himself as one of American brewing's first great marketing geniuses. An energetic whirlwind of innovation, Busch's accomplishments read like

Below: Some boys pause to feed the Clydesdale horses pulling the Budweiser brewery wagon in Charlotte, North Carolina. Anheuser-Busch is still well known for its Clydesdale teams, which make numerous public appearances around the United States. (*Library of Congress*)

a textbook of entrepreneurship. He launched a vigorous advertising campaign, formed a wide distribution network and set up ice houses on railroad sidings to keep long distance shipments of beer cool and fresh. Busch pioneered the new technology of artificial ice-making, and in 1877 he was the first brewer to ship his brew in refrigerated rail cars. He even owned his own railroad. Later, he helped pioneer the pasteurization of beer.

Busch was not the first to aspire to the notion of brewing a beer specially designed to appeal to people of all walks of life throughout the United States, but this was a goal that he would vigorously pursue. Along with his friend Carl Conrad, Busch created and introduced such a beer in 1876, America's centennial year. The two men considered the recipe and the name for this beer and the need for it to have broad appeal. The most popular brews of the day were those brewed in the manner of the lagers of central Europe's golden triangle (Bavaria-Austria-Bohemia). Many breweries produced brand names that alluded to that region. Indeed, the Anheuser-Busch Brewery had begun as George Schneider's "Bavarian" Brewery, but it was merely one of dozens of breweries that used the name "Bavarian." Of the golden lagers, the pale ones from the Bohemian corner of the triangle, the Pilsners, epitomized for Busch and Conrad the style they wanted.

Gerald Holland, writing in the October 1929 issue of *The American Mercury*, stated that it was Conrad who travelled to Europe and found the specific recipe in a specific Bohemian brewing city known in the Czech language as Ceske Budejovice. Since the city was then part of the Austro-Hungarian Empire, it was better known by its German name, Budweis. In the nineteenth century, as in the twenty-first century, the Budweis brewery brewed a beer that was called "Budweiser," just as beer brewed in Bavaria was called "Bavarian," beer from Prague was called "Prager," or as beer from Pilsen was (and is) called "Pilsner."

Adolphus Busch may or may not have had the Czech-speaking Bohemian town in mind when he chose "Budweiser" as the appellation of the beer that he planned to be his flagship brand. According to an Associated Press article appearing in the February 28, 2000 issue of *Modern Brewery Age* magazine, "Anheuser-Busch claims that it registered the Budweiser trademark in the United

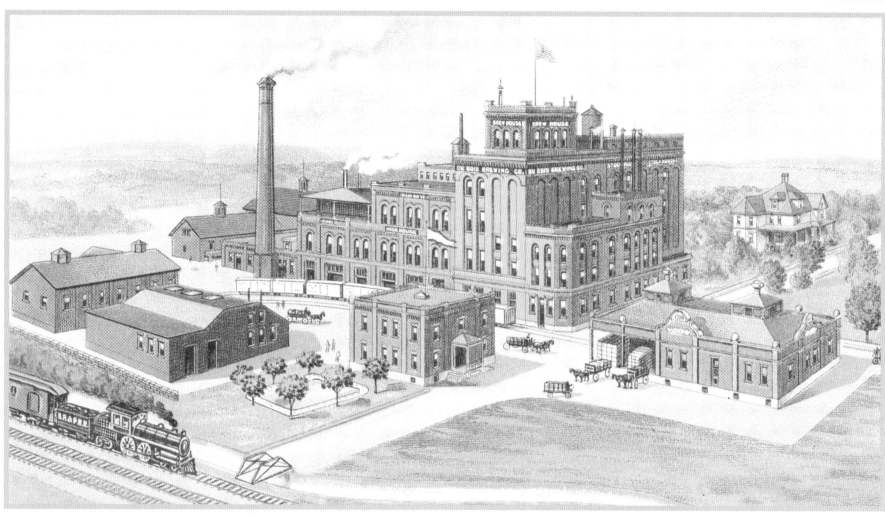

States in 1878, 19 years before the Czech brewery formally adopted the same name."

In a letter to trademark attorney Rowland Cox in 1894, Adolphus Busch stated that he selected the Budweiser name

Above: A classic view of the DuBois Brewery in the Pennsylvania city of the same name. Founded in 1897, it operated (except for Prohibition) until 1973. *(Collection of the author)*
Opposite: A Kentucky bartender, ready to serve. *(Courtesy of Carl Miller)*

Left: A waiter serves up a bottle of Budweiser. *(Library of Congress) Below:* To advertise their Falstaff brand, the Lemps commissioned this painting of Sir John holding court as everyone enjoyed a glass of beer. *(Collection of the author) Opposite:* The permanence represented by this bronze bust of Sir John Falstaff (emblazoned with the brewery insignia) tells us that the brand will not be forgotten. *(Bill Yenne photo)*

"because it was easily pronounceable by Americans and was not the name of any beer then sold in America."

Budweiser has not only survived as a brand name, it has prospered. By the latter part of the twentieth century, it had become the biggest-selling single brand in the United States and in the world, just as Anheuser-Busch later became the world's biggest brewing company. In 1896, Busch added another brand to his product line,

Michelob, which he described as being a "draught beer for connoisseurs." More than a century later, though overshadowed by Budweiser, Michelob remains an important Anheuser-Busch brand.

If George Schneider's brewery was the original building block of the brewing giant that became Anheuser-Busch, then the brewery founded by Wilhelm Stumpf in 1850 was the original building block of the *other* legendary name in St. Louis brewing — Falstaff.

The story of the Falstaff brand began with Johann Adam Lemp, a German brewer who arrived in St. Louis by way of Cincinnati in 1838. Two years later, Lemp started his first commercial brewery on South Second Street between Elm Street and Walnut Street. One of the first in the city to brew lager beer, Lemp was to become well known locally in 1845 for utilizing a cave complex south of St. Louis to "lager" or store his products. He harvested large quantities of ice from the Mississippi River in the winter, packed it into his caves and used it to keep his yeast at the proper temperature. Adam passed away in 1862, having transferred ownership of the brewery to his 25-year-old son, William Jacob Lemp, a year earlier. This plant was then operated

as the William J. Lemp & Company Western Brewery.

William's Western Brewery eventually became the city's largest, with a place in the top 20 nationally. It was larger even than Eberhard Anheuser's Bavarian Brewery before Adolphus Busch took over. Lemp and Busch would soon be the most powerful men in St. Louis brewing, as well as two of the city's most colorful characters. Together, they turned their city into a brewing center that rivaled Milwaukee.

Lemp was joined in business by his sons — Charles as company treasurer, Louis as the brewery superintendent, and William, Jr. as the corporate vice-president. In 1903, they picked a brand name. The name was that of Sir John Falstaff regarded as among the best-loved of William Shakespeare's characters. He was introduced as the archetypical "jolly sidekick" in *Henry VI*, and Queen Elizabeth loved him so much that she asked for more. Shakespeare obliged, casting him in a leading role in *The Merry Wives of Windsor*. He would appear in three plays and be mentioned in a fourth. Genial and generous, Sir John was a knight errant who was much more comfortable at a pun toss or quaffing ale at the Boar's Head Inn than knighting on

the battlefield or tournament. As a brewery mascot, however, he was not good luck for the Lemps.

In 1904, on the eve of the St. Louis World's Fair, the patriarch, William J. Lemp, committed suicide. Fourteen years later, another tragedy struck the Lemp Brewery — as well as the entire American brewing industry — Prohibition. In 1920, the last act taken by the Lemps before padlocking their brewery would be to sell the Falstaff trademark to a man named Joseph "Papa Joe" Griesedieck for $25,000.

Back in the 1860s, as William Lemp then undertook construction of a much larger brewery and storage facility on Cherokee Street near Carondelet Avenue, the German brewing brothers Anton and Heinrich Griesedieck arrived in St. Louis and started a brewery. Anton's son Joseph, later to be known as "Papa Joe," grew up in the brewery. In 1889, the elder Griesedieck's sold out in the huge British-financed industry consolidation that combined 18 breweries into the St. Louis Brewing Association. Afterward, however, they bounced back with a new operation called the National Brewery. In 1891, Papa Joe Griesedieck took over this facility, which would be his base of operations until 1906.

Left: Theodore Hamm. *(Bill Yenne Illustration)*
Below: Ludwig Hudepohl. *Below left:* A label from
Yoerg's Brewery *(Collection of the author)*

In that year, nine breweries united to become the Independent Breweries Company. Among them was the Griesedieck's National Brewery. The creators of this new consortium had chosen their name to distinguish a group of local companies from St. Louis Brewing Association, which had been formed 17 years before by the hand of the British venture capitalists. Both Lemp and Busch continued to remain independent, and in 1911, five years after the merger, Henry Griesedieck bought one of the nine components out of the Independent Breweries Company. It was not the former Griesedieck National Brewery, but the Consumers Brewing Company, which had been owned by the Lemps between 1860 and 1866, and by the Griesediecks from 1879 to 1882. Papa Joe, meanwhile, acquired the Forest Park Brewing Company in 1917. Anticipating Prohibition, he renamed it as the Griesedieck *Beverage* Company. In 1920, when he acquired the Falstaff trademark, Papa Joe renamed the company as the Falstaff Brewing Corporation.

In the late nineteenth century, as Milwaukee and St. Louis emerged to take their places along side New York as the great brewing centers in the United States, other important American brewing centers were seeing the rise of great brewing companies that would become household names, and remain so for most — if not all — of the twentieth century.

In Minnesota's twin cities of Minneapolis and St. Paul, an intercity rivalry defined the region's taste for beer for more than a century. Minneapolis Brewing & Malting originated in 1890, through a merger of the city's four largest brewing companies. Foremost among these was the brewery founded by John Orth in 1850. The others were Heinrich Brewing, dating back to 1866; Zahler & Noerenberg Brewing, founded by Anton Zahler in 1870; and Germania Brewing, which had been started in 1884. The huge brewery erected in 1892 on the site of Orth's brewery would soon be famous throughout the upper Midwest for its Grain Belt brand.

Across the Mississippi River in St. Paul, a German immigrant named Theodore Hamm acquired a four-year-old brewery started by Andrew Keller in 1860. By 1886, when William Hamm joined his father's company, it was the second largest brewing operation in Minnesota, with an annual production of 40,000 barrels. This compared with the paltry 500 barrels that the facility was doing when Theodore Hamm took over two decades earlier. Like

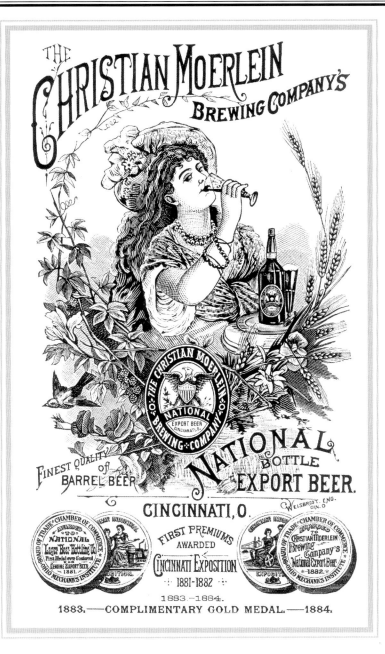

Left: An old Christian Moerlein poster. *(Collection of the author)*
Above: A Miller delivery wagon leaves the depot on the South Side of Chicago. *(Courtesy of the brewery) Right:* The people of Duluth are said to have chosen Stag. *(Collection of the author)*

Above: **Bernhard Stroh.** *(Bill Yenne illustration)* **Right: Workers at the Stroh Brewery in Detroit.** *(Collection of the author)*

the Grain Belt trademark, the Hamm name would soon become well known beyond the state.

The large German population in Cincinnati supported a number of sizable breweries. Indeed, by the 1890s, per capita beer consumption in Cincinnati was greater than in any other major United States city. Among the breweries satiating this thirst was that of Christian Moerlein. Started in 1853, it had become the eighth largest nationally by 1879. Another important Cincinnati regional was the Buckeye Brewery, founded on Buckeye Street in 1852 and acquired by Ludwig Hudepohl and George Kotte in 1885. The latter died in 1893, and Ludwig "Louis" Hudepohl II bought out his widow in 1900. Thereafter, Hudepohl Brewing emerged as a Cincinnati landmark. Unlike Moerlein, it survived Prohibition and flourished in mid-century — briefly reviving the Moerlein name as one of its brands.

In Detroit, the name that would emerge as the dominant regional brand was Stroh. Bernard (Bernhardt) Stroh started his brewery on Catherine Street in 1850, but moved twice, to Gratiot Avenue and later to Elizabeth Street. Between 1864 and 1882, the company was known as the Lion Brewery after the heraldic insignia that had always been part of the company logo and bottle labels. The Stroh name was readopted in 1882 and retained until the company folded in 1999. Throughout the latter nineteenth century and most of the twentieth, Stroh was Detroit's largest brewing company. In the 1980s, after having acquired Schlitz, Stroh became one of the top four brewing companies in the United States.

In the South, the second half of the nineteenth century was a time of "reconstruction" both in the political sense and in terms of infrastructure. In the case of the brewing industry, the region — except for Texas — would be largely devoid of major industrial-strength breweries until after World War II. No region of the country has had fewer breweries in its history, and one southern state, Mississippi, had never had a commercial brewery in its history until the era of the craft beer revolution.

One exception in the deep South was the city of New Orleans. Three small brewery owners who had been doing business in the 1850s — Joseph Christen, L. Fasnacht and George Mertz — reopened after the Civil War, and they were joined by eight others within

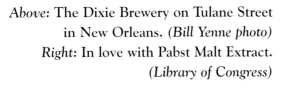

Above: The Dixie Brewery on Tulane Street in New Orleans. *(Bill Yenne photo)*
Right: In love with Pabst Malt Extract. *(Library of Congress)*

Right: An old newspaper ad for the Lone Star Brewing Company. *(Collection of the author)* *Below and opposite:* The Tivoli Union Brewery in Denver, Colorado had that kind of classic brewery architecture that always elicited a double take. *(Library of Congress)*

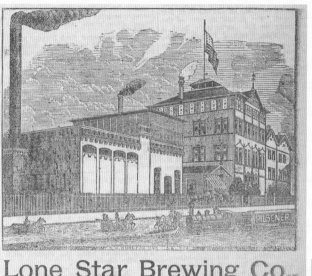

Lone Star Brewing Co.,
San Antonio, Texas.

five years. Big breweries on the scale of those that existed in the North appeared in New Orleans around the turn of the century. These included the Jackson Brewery on Decatur Street in the French Quarter, opened in 1890 and the Dixie Brewery, which opened on Tulane Street in 1907. The Jackson Brewery — and its signature brand, Jax Beer — would survive until 1974, but the Dixie Brewing Company would still be extant in the twenty-first century.

In Texas, there had been a great influx of German immigrants, especially in San Antonio. Two of the most important breweries were the one started on the north side of town by J.B. Behloradsky in 1881, and the Lone Star Brewery, started on the south side in 1884 by Adolphus Busch. Though Busch also owned Anheuser-Busch, Lone Star would be held separately. The brewery closed with Prohibition, although the name was revived at a new site in the 1930s. Behloradsky's brewery, known simply as San Antonio Brewing after 1883, began using the Pearl Beer brand name in 1886, and officially became Pearl Brewing in 1952.

In the town of Shiner, located about an hour east of San Antonio, the Shiner Brewing Association was started in 1909. It was taken over by the Betzold and Spoetzl partnership in 1915. Known as the Spoetzl Brewery, it would survive Prohibition and end the twentieth century as the oldest surviving independent brewery in the Lone Star State.

The Rocky Mountain West saw the emergence of two

major regional brewing centers during the latter half of the nineteenth century. Not surprisingly, these areas were also emerging as major mining centers for gold and other precious metals. The two centers were the Denver area in Colorado Territory and the Anaconda-Butte-Helena triangle in Montana Territory. Denver's first brewery, the Rocky Mountain Brewery on Cherry Creek, was taken over by early Colorado pioneer John Good in 1861, two years after in was started. A master brewer from Europe, Good had arrived in 1859 with one of the first wagon trains bound for Denver. After a year of being in partnership with Philip Zang, Good moved on and the company became Philip Zang Brewing, which flourished until Prohibition. Good's next move was to Aspen, where he operated in an off-and-on partnership with Jacob Mack through the 1880s and 1890s.

In 1900, Good took control of a Denver brewery called the Milwaukee Brewery, which had been founded in 1864 and operated since 1879 by Max Melsheimer and John Mack. Good renamed the enterprise as the Tivoli Brewery, named after Tivoli Gardens in Copenhagen. Known as the Western Products Company during Prohibition, it re-emerged as Tivoli Union in 1934. The "Union" suffix was dropped in 1953, and for six years beginning in 1958, it was also known as the Mountain Brewing Company. The company remained under the ownership of the Good family and their descendants until 1965.

About a half day's ride from Denver, the town of Golden, Colorado got its first brewery, the Golden City, in 1868, but it folded in 1874. In the meantime, its second brewing company, the Golden Brewery, was started in 1873 by Jacob Schueler and Adolph Coors. The latter had apprenticed to several breweries in Germany before emigrating to the United States in 1868 at the age of 21. After a stint at the Stenger Brewery in Naperville, Illinois, he headed west to Colorado. Coors and Schueler became successful in the gold fields not by mining, but by providing the gold miners with golden lager. Coors bought out his partner in 1880 and by 1890, Coors Brewing & Malting was producing 17,600 barrels annually, a five-fold increase over the 1880 output.

In 1863, the year before Montana became a territory with Virginia City as its capital, Thomas Smith started the first brewery in the city. In 1874, Helena replaced Virginia City as the territorial capital and in 1883, the Northern Pacific

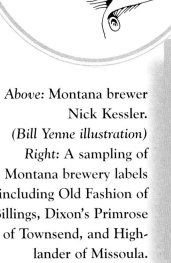

Above: **Montana brewer Nick Kessler.**
(Bill Yenne illustration)
Right: A sampling of Montana brewery labels including Old Fashion of Billings, Dixon's Primrose of Townsend, and Highlander of Missoula.
(Collection of the author)

Railroad linked Montana's rich mining towns with the outside world. It was in Helena that one of the state's most famous breweries had been founded. Started by Charles Beehrer in 1864, it was taken over two years later by Nicholas Kessler, an immigrant from Luxembourg. In 1886, Kessler built a new brewery on the site that included the first refrigeration unit ever used in Montana and the first carbonic acid machine installed in a United States brewery. Kessler died in 1901, but the brewery would operate until 1958. In 1982, the Kessler brand was revived in Helena by a microbrewery operation known as Montana Beverages.

Leopold Friedreich Schmidt was to Butte, Montana's metropolis, what Nick Kessler was to the state capital. As with many young men of his era, he was bitten by the gold bug, and he eventually travelled into the Mountain West in search of opportunities in the mines and placers. He came to Butte in search of one kind of gold, but found another — lager. In 1876, America's centennial year, Schmidt founded what would be known as the Centennial Brewery. Schmidt's operation was Butte's first major commercial brewery and a major success story.

Schmidt became one of Butte's leading citizens, and, as was expected of leading citizens, he served a couple of terms in the Montana legislature. In 1889, both Washington and Montana Territories were scheduled to enter the union as states. In the course of his duties as a state official, Leopold Schmidt travelled to the Washington capital in Olympia, at the southern end of Puget Sound. While in Washington, Schmidt discovered the natural artesian waters located in the little town of Tumwater, immediately south of Olympia. He had it tested and decided that this was the perfect water for brewing, so he moved his family and base of operations west. He bought property for the new brewery in

Tumwater on the Deschutes River at Lower Tumwater Falls.

In 1896, Schmidt opened his Capital Brewing Company, kegging the first brew on the first of October. In 1902, the company was renamed as the Olympia Brewing Company. By now, Schmidt's beer was popular throughout the Northwest, especially in the growing metropolis of Seattle.

Meanwhile, Schmidt's Centennial Brewery in Butte was sold to Henry Mueller in 1897, and closed permanently in 1918 on the eve of Prohibition, but the Olympia brewery would survive past the end of the twentieth century. In 1906, Schmidt built a grand new brick brewery building on his Tumwater property. Though this building would become the symbol of the Olympia Brewing Company, it would be the actual Olympia brewery for just eight years.

North of Olympia on Puget Sound, Seattle in the nineteenth century was quickly growing into Washington's major city. The major metropolis of the Pacific Northwest, Seattle grew up fast as a center of both the lumbering and fishing industries. Both loggers and fisherman grew thirsty and the brewing industry naturally followed. A.B. Rabbeson's Washington Brewery had been the first in 1854, and it became the Seattle Brewery in 1872, which would survive until 1888. By this time, especially during the 1880s, a number of other brewers had come on the scene. The operation begun by John Kopp and Andrew Hemrich in 1883 became Seattle Brewing & Malting. Best known as "The House of Hemrich," it swallowed up five other Seattle breweries between 1892 and 1904. Between 1906 and 1915, the company developed the well known brand name Rainier, named for Mount Rainier, the snow-capped 14,410-foot volcanic peak that is visible from Seattle.

As Seattle became the metropolis and brewing center of the Pacific Northwest in the latter nineteenth century, San Francisco had become these for California before the Civil War. San Franciscans had developed a reputation for being self-sufficient and self-reliant. Until the completion of the Transcontinental Railroad in 1869, they were cut off from the rest of the United States by a treacherous ocean voyage that could take up to half a year. Self-reliance meant that San Francisco had become a brewing center whose importance rivaled that of Cincinnati or St. Louis.

An interesting footnote to San Francisco brewing is that while Eastern brew-

Above: **A Victorian-era, "Gibson Girl" Olympia serving tray observed in an old tavern in the Pacific Northwest.** (*Bill Yenne photo*)

Left: San Francisco brewer John Wieland. *(Bill Yenne illustration) Below:* Beer labels from San Francisco and San Diego. The California Brewing Association was a forerunner to the Acme brand. *(Collection of the author) Right and facing page inset:* Otto Schinkel and Ernst Baruth, proprietors of the Anchor Brewery. *(Courtesy of Anchor Brewing Company). Facing page:* An early photo of the of the Anchor Brewery. *(Courtesy of Anchor Brewing Company)*

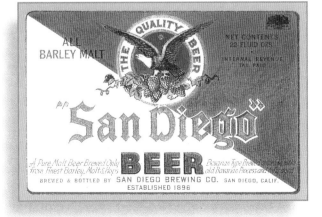

eries were often named after cities and regions in Germany and Central Europe, breweries in the West often were named after brewing centers in the East. San Francisco had a "Philadelphia Brewery," and, like Denver and other Western cities, San Francisco had a "Milwaukee Brewery." San Francisco's Milwaukee Brewery on Seventh Street was started in 1868 and, having survived Prohibition, it would be restarted in 1935 and renamed as the San Francisco Brewing Corporation.

Some of San Francisco's notable breweries included those started by Charles Wilmot on Telegraph Hill in 1856 and John Wieland's Philadelphia Brewery on Second Street, which was founded the same year. The latter became John Wieland Brewing in 1887 and was one of the West's most important breweries by the turn of the century. Another prominent San Francisco brewing company was the National Brewery, established by John Glueck and Charles Hansen at Fulton and Webster in 1861, which would achieve a great deal of fame in the middle twentieth century for its well-known Acme brand.

The brand that is most closely associated with San Francisco today was born in 1896, German brewer Ernst F. Baruth and his son-in-law, Otto Schinkel, Jr., bought the old brewery on Pacific Avenue that was started by Gottlieb Brekle in the Gold Rush era, and renamed it as the Anchor Brewery. Baruth and his previous partner, Henry C. Kroenke, had been co-owners of the American Brewery on Green Street. No one knows why Baruth and Schinkel chose the name Anchor, except, perhaps, for its indirect but powerful allusion to the great Port of San Francisco.

The latter years of the nineteenth century were important for the maturing United States brewing industry. The trends were two-fold. First, there was an increase in the overall output of the industries, and second, there was a drop in the total number of breweries doing the producing.

The number of breweries in operation in the United States hit its all-time apogee of 4,131 in 1873, but just seven years later, by the reckoning of the Internal Revenue Department, which taxed the breweries, the number had dropped to 2,830 breweries in operation. At the same time, however, the annual output of the industry increased from 9.6 million to 13.3 million barrels in 1880. This meant that the average output per brewery doubled from 2,324 barrels to 4,700 barrels. By 1890, the total industry output had more than doubled again to 27.6 million barrels, and Pabst became the first single brewing company to exceed a million barrels annually on its own.

Part of the success story of American brewing at the end of the nineteenth century had to do with efficiencies of production. Brewing was becoming more of a science than an art, as equipment — such as instrumentation for measuring original

Left: **Even in the nineteenth century, scientists understood that brown glass protected beer. Schlitz pointed this out to distance itself from rivals who used clear glass.** *Below:* **Pawnee Dark from Columbus Brewing.** *(Collection of the author)* *Below right:* **A Miller Brewing distribution center in Milwaukee.** *(Courtesy of the brewery)*

gravity, the density of wort — became more sophisticated. For example, when Danish brewing chemists, led by Emil Christian Hansen, isolated the *Saccharomyces carlsbergensis* yeast strain in 1883, they not only changed an industry, they helped to originate the entire field of molecular biology.

Part of the story was efficiencies in such simple things as packaging. Before the Civil War, bottle making was a com-

plex and cumbersome process. By the end of the century, bottles were mass produced. The invention of the now-common crown cap — by William Painter of Crown Cork and Seal in Baltimore — in 1892, revolutionized bottling, speeding up the process and reducing costs tremendously.

Another part of the story had to do with the efficiencies of transportation. Reaching 193,346 miles by the turn of the century — nearly four times its size in

1870 — the American rail network would provide immense opportunity for a new generation of entrepreneur brewers who would begin dreaming the dream of national brands. It was not only the fact that the rail network was so large, it was the fact that it was so comprehensive. Thanks to competition for freight among the railroads, virtually every corner of the country was connected to every other. Thanks to competition for the consumers' dollar, virtually every corner of the country had fresh beer delivered from a strong regional or local brewery.

The expansion of the United States brewing industry in the half century after the Civil War mirrored the expanding economy of the nation as a whole. Even in the aftermath of the Panics (recessions) of 1873 and 1893, people wanted a beer. The mega-brewers in major centers such as Milwaukee and New York City grew, working hard to satisfy the growing national thirst. So too did the smaller, but robust regionals from San Francisco to New Orleans. The late nineteenth century was a good time for the brewing industry, and it was a good time for consumers as well, as fresh beer and a variety of styles were more widely available than at any time in the past.

Above: Mathkirar's Tavern proudly associated itself with the Miller High Life brand. *(Courtesy of the brewery)*

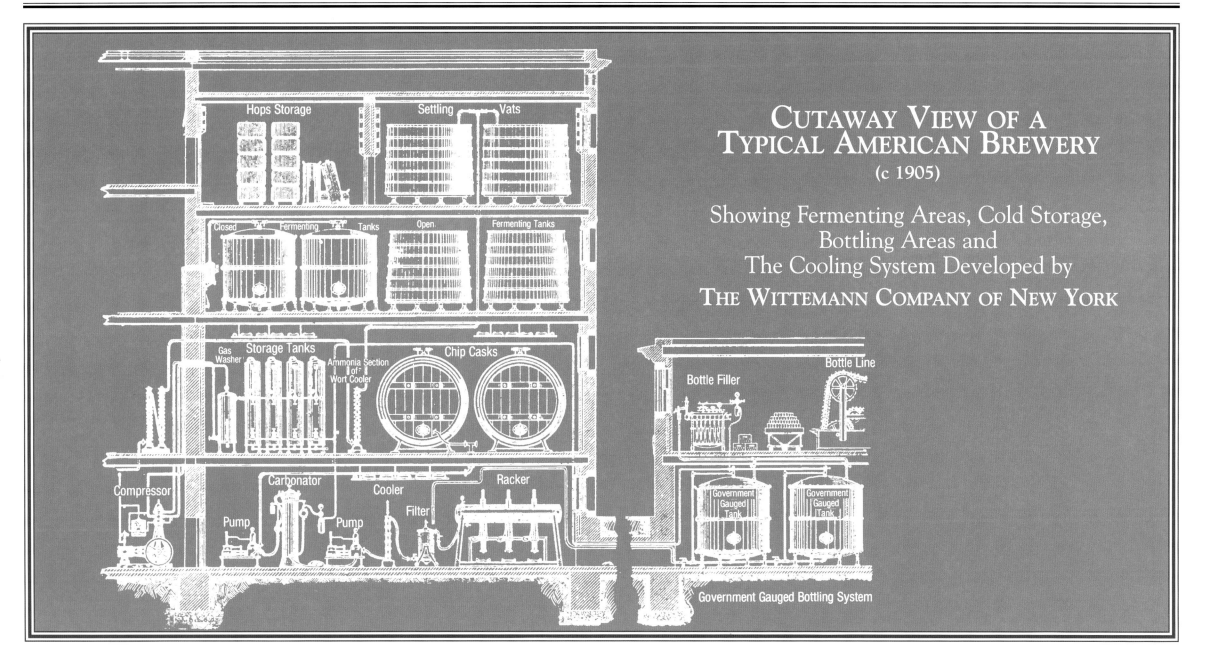

CUTAWAY VIEW OF A
TYPICAL AMERICAN BREWERY
(c 1905)

Showing Fermenting Areas, Cold Storage,
Bottling Areas and
The Cooling System Developed by
THE WITTEMANN COMPANY OF NEW YORK

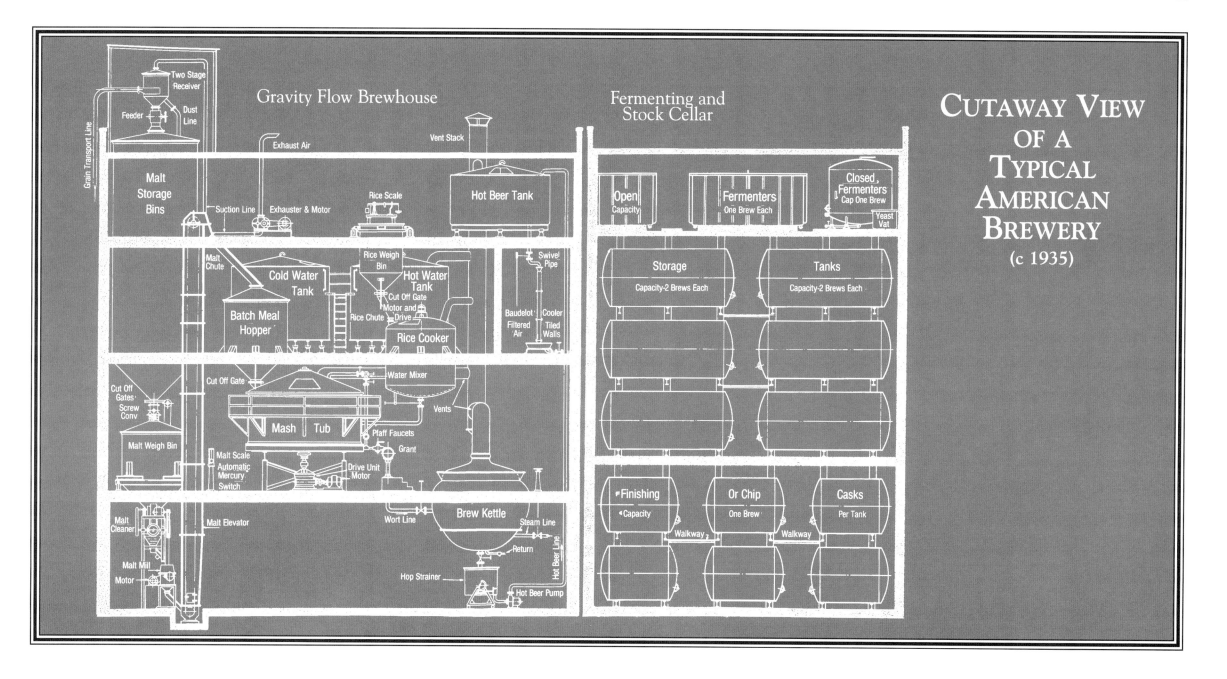

CUTAWAY VIEW OF A TYPICAL AMERICAN BREWERY (c 1935)

Chapter 4

INTO THE TWENTIETH CENTURY

AS THE NEW CENTURY BEGAN, THE population of the United States reached 76 million, having doubled since the end of the Civil War. Meanwhile, the annual output of the United States brewing industry increased tenfold from 3.7 million barrels in 1865 to 39.5 million in 1900. In fact, the industry's 1900 production was up an amazing 43 percent since 1890. Pabst, the first American brewer to top a million barrels annually, was itself topped by cross-town rival, Joseph Schlitz. Now there were a pair of million-barrel brewers and soon there would be more. Schlitz was also an early pioneer in multi-site brewing. In 1908, the company built a satellite brewery in Cleveland, Ohio from scratch.

It was a time of expansiveness and it was a time of growing brand consciousness. Captain Pabst was tying blue silk ribbons onto bottles of Blue Ribbon beer, and the Lemps were preparing to launch their Falstaff brand in time for the 1904 St. Louis World's Fair. In Milwaukee, the Miller Brewing Company officially rolled out what would long be its flagship brand, Miller High Life, amid great fanfare on December 30, 1903. Frederick Miller's son, Ernst Miller, had the idea to position it as a stylish product for the most elite of consumers. To underscore this, the Miller High Life slogan was coined in 1906, and

Miller High Life became the "Champagne of Bottle Beer."

As a trademark for Miller High Life, the company adopted the famous "Girl in the Moon." First used in advertising during 1904, she became one of most recognized trademarks in American brewing history. The mysterious woman was rumored to have been the daughter of someone important, and from time to time, a woman has come forward to assert that *she* was the mystery girl. In fact, she was discovered in 1902 by Albert C. Paul, who was then the advertising and marketing manager at Miller Brewing. Described in period accounts as "a Mexican señorita," she was carved into a ten-inch piece of wood from an old wooden box that was not a beer crate. Though she had long been known as the "Girl in the Moon," A.C. Paul did not actually place her on the moon until 1907.

In the heady days of the first decade of the twentieth century, as consumers sipped their lager to the tune of ragtime music, the brewing industry was continuing to evolve. Even as total production increased, the number of breweries was declining more rapidly than ever. From a peak of more than 4,000 in 1873 to fewer than half that number early in the twenti-

No. 4002.   You Auto see Milwaukee.

Above: Milwaukee in 1908, a beer-lovers' theme park. *Opposite:* Stroh Brewery trucks roll into the new century. *(Collection of the author)*

Above: The Brauhaus on 86th Street was the epicenter of beer, fun and German food in New York City. Most US cities had such places. (*Collection of the author*)
Right: The Girl in the Moon has been the mystery girl of Miller High Life for more than a century. (*Courtesy of the brewery*) *Opposite:* Enjoying a touch of nostalgia at Menominee River Brewing in Michigan. (*Collection of the author*)

eth century. The reason was obviously not a lack of interest in the product, but a phenomenon that affects most industries periodically — consolidation. In 1889, British venture capitalists unsuccessfully attempted a takeover and consolidation of Pabst, Schlitz and Blatz in Milwaukee, but a similar effort that same year succeeded in consolidating 18 breweries in St. Louis into an entity that would be called the St. Louis Brewing Association. The following year, a half dozen companies in New Orleans were merged into a single entity.

In the first few years of the new century, 10 Boston-area companies became the Massachusetts Breweries Company and 16 independent brewing companies in Baltimore merged, taking the name of the biggest three as the Gottlieb-Bauernschmidt-Straus Brewing Company. Meanwhile, in 1899, 21 western Pennsylvania brewers were combined to

form the Pittsburgh Brewing Company. In 1905, another 15 brewing companies in Pittsburgh moved to counter the former merger, uniting as the Independent Brewing Company. In just these few examples, 86 breweries were replaced by just a half dozen brewing companies.

However, other changes were in the wind. Even as the industry was enjoying record years, the dark clouds of Prohibition were gathering on the distant horizon and were drawing nearer. Writing in 1909, G. Thomann of the United States Brewers' Association observed a slowing of the annual increases. He observed the remarkable increases in the years 1906 and 1907, amounting respectively to 5,129,607 and 3,970,362 barrels, comparing it to "a very insignificant increase of 192,031 in 1908."

He attributed part of this trend to the current economic downturn, but saw more sinister trends afoot. "The greater part of this loss is doubtless due to the [recession of 1907], but it is quite certain that a considerable proportion of the decrease was caused directly by Prohibition of one form or another," said Thomann. "It is difficult to localize these losses with mathematical accuracy, but there can be no doubt that brewing has suffered in all parts of the country where the Anti-Saloon movement has succeeded. From present indications it is safe to infer that in the South the industry will in the end suffer more than anywhere else; it is equally certain, however, that, unless the adverse movement should develop greater strength than appears probable at the present time, brewing throughout the country will rapidly recover from its recent setback and resume its former rate of development, acquiring new markets and new customers as has been the case during the [past] fifty years."

As Thomann points out, some of the states had already passed various forms of restrictive legislation during the nineteenth century, but by the early twentieth century, Prohibition became a national political issue.

Though it had been percolating in subcultures of society for a long time, the move toward Prohibition began gaining momentum in the late nineteenth century. Originally a religious-based sentiment, it became political as various radical organizations, such as the notorious Anti-Saloon League, to which Thomann refers, became involved. Operating under the banner of the so-called "temperance movement," they demanded that government take a role in regulating personal interests. The League was founded in 1893 in Oberlin,

Below: Detroit police inspecting equipment found in a clandestine underground brewery during the dark days of Prohibition. *(National Archives)* **Opposite:** Elizabeth Thompson, a proud member of the Crusaders, crusading for Repeal. *(Library of Congress)*

Ohio by Reverend Howard Hyde Russell and representatives of various temperance societies and evangelical, anti-Catholic churches. Later spearheaded by James Cannon, Jr., a Methodist bishop, the League turned the temperance flame into a bonfire that destroyed the livelihoods of many of the families that it pretended to want to save. In Milwaukee alone, at least 6,500 brewery employees would lose their careers because of Russell and his followers.

Prohibition was an earthquake that decimated both an industry and a great cultural tradition — the hometown brewer. Now regarded as one of the worst legislative disasters in United States history, Prohibition was undertaken with respectable intentions and was even described at the time as "The Noble Experiment."

There was a decidedly bigoted dimension to the temperance movement, pursued by many as an excuse to justify hatred of minorities. Because beer and wine were associated with immigrant cultures, especially the Germans, Irish, and Italians, many joined the temperance movement out of a belief that alcohol was an indulgence of inferior races. One would have liked to have had George Washington and Thomas Jefferson around to rebut this notion.

Eventually, Prohibitionism would also help to revive the Ku Klux Klan, which had flourished immediately after the Civil War, but which had become moribund by the turn of the century. Glad to be active again, the Klansmen energetically climbed aboard the bandwagon to campaign against Catholics and any others who were ethnically predisposed to be corrupted by "loose morals." In the South, where alcohol abuse was often seen as the catalyst for African-American "misbehavior," the Klan was swift to act.

Thomann wrote at an especially dark moment in American brewing history. After complaining about lesser and lesser *increases*, total production actually *declined* by 2.4 million barrels to 56.3 million in 1909, but it bounced back in 1910 to 59.5 million. Although annual output hit an all-time high of 66.2 million barrels in 1914, sales then sagged, and next, collapsed. They would not exceed the 1914 high until 1943.

World War I, which began in Europe in 1914 and swept up the United States in 1917, saw the brewing industry increasingly targeted by ethnic bigotry. Prohibitionists used anti-German sentiment against the owners of breweries, mainly in the upper Midwest, most of whom were German. German-Americans working in the brewing industry — even those whose parents were born in the United States — were openly derided as traitors for producing "Kaiser Brew." The radicals also used the need to keep factory workers sober as an excuse to promote their agenda.

By the time that a constitutional amendment to prohibit the manufacture and sale of alcoholic beverages in the United States had passed Congress at the end of 1917, two dozen states had already gone "dry." Ratified as the 18th Amendment, Prohibition became law in January 1920. It was enforced by the draconian Volstead Act of 1919. Under Prohibition, it became illegal to manufacture, transport, or sell alcoholic beverages in the United States.

Breweries that had been legitimate family businesses one day, became empty shells the next. Many of the larger brewing companies turned to other products. Those who owned malting facilities were able to convert to cereal products. Others turned to brewing non-alcoholic "near beer." Because real beer was never far from near beer, a tongue in cheek slogan cropped up: "Near Beer Sold Here. Real Beer Sold Near Here." This illustrated the fact that, while legitimate businesses suffered, illegal production was rampant. With alcoholic beverages banned, their manufacture became a growth industry for gangsters such as Al Capone.

The major companies who had once led the industry, now promoted their brands of near beer. Anheuser-Busch had its Bevo, Miller marketed Vivo, and Coors, one of the only brewers left in Colorado, chose the auspicious name, Mannah. Anheuser-Busch also produced a coffee-flavored Kafo and a chocolate-flavored Carcho. Schlitz, banned from brewing "the beer that made Milwaukee famous," now hoped to make the city famous with a product called Famo. Pabst, meanwhile, trademarked three peculiar brand names, Hoppy, Pablo and Yip. Both Stroh in Detroit and Weinhard in Oregon used the name Luxo. On the Hamm's product list was the Digesto Brand malt extract, which the company had been marketing to "nursing mothers" and "tired housewives" since the early 1900s.

The annual output of the United States brewing industry dropped from 66.2 million barrels in 1914 to 27.7 million barrels in 1919, the last year that beer was legal. That was the lowest volume since 1890. It certainly didn't help that the federal government doubled the tax from three to six dollars a barrel in 1919. In 1920, the industry produced only 9.3 million barrels of near beer, but that number declined every year thereafter to a mere 2.8 million barrels in 1932, the last full year of Prohibition.

The "Noble Experiment" had become an ignoble disaster. Against the backdrop of the bootlegging culture of the "Roaring Twenties," it was obvious that the experiment had failed. In 1932, a plank in Franklin D. Roosevelt's presidential campaign platform called for "Repeal." He won in a landslide. Within a month of his inauguration in 1933, he signed "emergency" legislation legalizing beer. Though Repeal was not fully implemented through the 21st Amendment until December 1933, Roosevelt "got the *beer* flowing" in most states in April.

After Repeal, the industry struggled to gain its feet. The major companies that had stayed afloat with near beer and other products were able to resume brewing within a short time, but smaller businesses found resumption to be a bit more difficult. Many of the small town breweries that had folded, stayed folded. Of the 1,568 breweries that had existed in 1920, only 756 would reopen, and most of these would cease to exist during the ensuing Great Depression. Because of the weight of expenses incurred in reopening, many of those that restarted would fail during the first year after Repeal.

In 1933, the industry produced 11 million barrels of real beer, nearly four times the volume of near beer produced the previous year. The industry worked to shake off the detrimental effects of more than 14 years of darkness, facing a myriad of difficulties that ranged from technical production issues to reopening a long moribund marketing network. Nevertheless, 1934 surpassed 1919 by 10 million barrels, reaching 37.7 million. The following year, the number was up to 45.2 million. The industry that reopened in 1933-1934 was clearly older and wiser. As at the time of the Civil War, leading brewers clearly saw the need to organize to protect their industry. New professional associations and business organizations formed throughout the country would merge in

1941 as the United States Brewers's Association.

New technology also came on line. Originally, beer had been tapped from barrels to be poured into glasses in taverns or into buckets for job sites. During the nineteenth century, bottled beer had become common, and in the 1890s, crown caps made bottling easier and cheaper. By 1935, advances in packaging led brewers to begin canning beer. Krueger Brewing of Newark was the first, using a flat-topped can that was the shape of a modern beer can. Pabst was also among the first to offer canned beer, and the first to use a new easy to use metal keg. The canned beer would, for a time, be marketed as Pabst Export Beer. The name Pabst Blue Ribbon would be reserved for the bottled product until the end of the decade. Schlitz soon followed suit with a "cone-top" can developed by the Continental Can Company that gave the impression of being shaped like a bottle. Pabst re-introduced Pabst Blue Ribbon Beer — briefly marketed again with the actual cloth ribbon — and the beer quickly resumed its position of prominence among consumers. In 1933, to meet demand in the early years after Repeal, Pabst purchased the Premier Malt

Left: Three lumbermen enjoy their Falstaffs. (*Collection of the author*) *Opposite:* Marching for their rights! (*Library of Congress*)

Above and left: Nicely designed 1930s-vintage labels from the Weber and Enterprise breweries. (*Collection of the author*)

Above: **A smart and stylish host entertains with Schlitz, and his guests are pleased.** *(Collection of the author) Opposite:* **A group of equally stylish folks happily toast the new dawn that was represented by Repeal.** *(Library of Congress)*

Products company, a Prohibition-era start-up in Peoria Heights, Illinois. With this, the official corporate name would be the hyphenated "Premier-Pabst Corporation." In 1938, the word Premier would be dropped.

The advent of canned beer, and greater efficiencies in bottling and transporting packaged beer led to a major shift in how beer was drunk by consumers. In the nineteenth century and the early twentieth century, beer was typically enjoyed on draft in dining establishments and at the neighborhood tavern. Indeed, as late as 1934, the first full year after Repeal, an industry survey showed that 75 percent of beer was still sold on draft. Only three years later, that proportion had declined to 56 percent. After World War II, as drinking habits continued to change, only a third of beer sold in the United States was on draft.

In the 1930s, as the regional breweries set out to reclaim their regions and make them larger, brands such as Schlitz, Pabst and Anheuser-Busch's Budweiser were now approaching the sta-

tus of national brands. With these three companies, the list of the top six American breweries was rounded out by three regionals in the largest single market in the United States — New York City. These were Ballantine, Schaefer and a new name, Ruppert.

A new king had been crowned in New York. George Ehret had passed away in 1927, seven years into Prohibition, leaving an estate of $40 million. In 1935, his family sold the moribund brewery site in Manhattan to Colonel Jacob Ruppert, an up-and-coming brewing industry figure. In 1936, George's son Louis would go back into the brewing business in Brooklyn, but he never achieved the success of his father. In 1948, he transferred his operations to the old Palisade Brewery site in Union City, New Jersey, but this was folded just two years later.

The colonel was a colorful character who had been born to privilege on Manhattan's upper east side in 1867. His father's brewery, founded in the year that Jacob was born, was located on Third Avenue, not far from Ehret's big brewery. As a young man, Jacob served for a time as an aide in the New York governor's office, where he was given the honorary rank of colonel, a title he would use for the rest of his life. By the turn of the century, the colonel had taken over the family brewing business, already famous for its Knickerbocker brand. By the time that Prohibition ended, the Ruppert Brewery had joined Schaefer and Ballantine as one of the big three in the New York City metropolitan area, and the only one of the group still brewing in Manhattan.

His own greatest fame in New York City came to Ruppert after he bought the New York Yankees baseball club in 1915. He turned a marginal team into a legend by hiring players such as Babe Ruth, Lou Gehrig — and much later, Joe DiMaggio, the "Yankee Clipper." Yankee Stadium, known as the "house that Ruth built," was actually built by Colonel Jacob Ruppert. The Yankees dominated baseball during the quarter century that the colonel owned the team, winning the World Series seven times. When Ruppert died on Friday the 13th of January 1939, more than 4,000 people turned out for his funeral at St. Patrick's Cathedral.

In linking beer with baseball on a corporate level, Ruppert pioneered a phenomenon that would become standard practice after World War II, that is formal sponsorship of the national pastime by brewing companies. As Stanley Baron,

make mine RUPPERT

Tasting is Believing

Left: **Taking a break from the tennis court to enjoy a cold Ruppert.** *Below*: **Featured on the cover of the brewery's calendar, Santa's elves enjoy their Ruppert break.** (*Courtesy of Joe Radman*)

WITH OUR SINCERE WISH FOR A
Merry Christmas and a Happy New Year
FOR YOU AND YOURS

wrote in his 1962 book *Brewed in America*, "Presumably Ruppert bought the club because of his love for baseball and especially the Yankees, rather than for any benefit he thought his brewery might derive from the association, but in any case his action created a highly favorable attitude toward beer and the industry — one which brewers since then have been wise to enhance."

While Ruppert's name dominated New York in the 1930s, old names such as Schaefer and Ballantine were still around, although the latter had undergone an abrupt consolidation during Prohibition. The huge brewing plant on Front Street, where Peter Ballantine had first brewed ale eight decades before, was closed — while the former Schalk brewery on Freeman Street would keep the company alive by manufacturing malt syrup. Gradually many of the family members who

would have joined the company if not for Prohibition drifted away to pursue other interests.

After Repeal, the Ballantine family was ready to sell. It had been one century since Peter Ballantine had first gone into business. Ironically, the new owners of nineteenth century's last great English-style brewery in America would be German. Otto and Carl W. Badenhausen had made their fortune selling brewery supplies in South America and were ready to start brewing themselves. The brothers did, however, pay their respects to Ballantine's heritage by importing a Scottish brewmaster.

During the 1930s, Ballantine came back to prominence and by 1940, the company was in the top six nationally. Carl W. Badenhausen himself had become such a respected member of the industry that he was named chairman of the United Brewers' Industrial Foundation, later known as the United States Brewers's Foundation.

Across the continent in Seattle, the mirror image of Jacob Ruppert was a man named Emil Sick. Both men brewed a locally popular beer, and both were associated with a pro baseball team. Ruppert owned the New York Yankees of the

American League from 1915 until his death in 1939. Emil Sick owned the Seattle Rainiers of the Pacific Coast League from 1938 until 1960. Of course, the notion of brewers owning baseball clubs was not confined to Ruppert and Sick. In 1953, Anheuser-Busch would become the owner of their home town St. Louis Cardinals.

Both men became important players in their regions, but while Ruppert's was in a metropolitan area, Sick operated breweries in three states — Washington, Oregon, Montana — plus the Canadian province of Alberta. Both men inherited their breweries from their fathers. Fritz Sick had started the Lethbridge Brewing & Malting Company in Lethbridge, Alberta, Canada in 1901. Emil took over from his father and used the Lethbridge brewery as a springboard for his American empire. After Repeal, Emil acquired the defunct Seattle Brewing & Malting, best known for the popular Rainier brand. In 1935, without having actually started brewing at Seattle Brewing & Malting, Sick bought Century Brewing across town. Operating this plant as Seattle Brewing & Malting, he re-launched the Rainier brand, which soon would become a household word throughout the entire Pacific Northwest.

In 1940, Sick bought the Spokane Brewery — across the state, in the city of the same name — which had been started

Left and above: Entertaining in New York during the 1940s meant serving your guests Ruppert Beer. (*Courtesy of Joe Radman*)

Left and below: **Highlander and Rainier labels from the Missoula and Seattle corners of the Emil Sick empire are overlayed on a photo of the Seattle Brewing & Malting plant on Airport Way in the Emerald City.** *(Collection of the author)*

by Galland-Burke in 1892. It would be known as Sick's Rainier Brewery of Spokane after 1958. In 1943, Emil acquired the Salem Brewery in Oregon's state capital, which had been started by Samuel Adolph in 1874. In Montana, just across the border from Lethbridge, Alberta, Emil Sick bought two breweries in 1944. These were Missoula Brewing which had been started by George Gerber in 1874 and Great Falls Breweries, which had originated in 1895 as American Brewing. With the Missoula and Great Falls acquisitions, Sick took possession of the two most prominent brand names in Montana, Highlander and Great Falls Select. Indeed Highlander was so prominent, that it would also be brewed at the Rainier plant in Seattle. Sick also operated a Rainier Brewery in San Francisco in a plant that his father bought just before prohibition.

In St. Louis, across town from Anheuser-Busch, Falstaff had literally been the first brewery to emerge from Prohibition. When Franklin Roosevelt signed the legislation that allowed for emergency permits authorizing the resumption of beer production in April 1933, Permit Number One was issued to none other than Papa Joe Griesedieck. Having grown up watching the effects of the great St. Louis brewery consolidations of 1889 and 1906, Papa Joe saw this strategy as the road to his own future success. In 1933, just a matter of weeks after he received his permit, he acquired Otto Stifel's Union Brewery on Michigan Avenue and incorporated it into his empire as Falstaff Brewing Corporation Plant Two.

In 1934, with two facilities running in St. Louis, Papa Joe looked south to New

Orleans, where he acquired the National Brewing Company, founded in 1911. In 1937, Papa Joe turned west to Omaha, Nebraska and purchased the brewery started by Fred Krug in 1859. The two properties both ran up the flag of the Falstaff Brewing Company, and Papa Joe became the first major brewing magnate to operate breweries in three separate states. In a few short years since Repeal, he had established Falstaff as one of the preeminent beer brands in America. When Papa Joe died in 1938 at the age of 75, his son, Alvin Griesedieck, took over the breweries of the Falstaff empire, demonstrating an energy and business acumen that would have made Papa Joe proud.

Meanwhile, Papa Joe's cousin, Henry L. Griesedieck, crossed the Mississippi River into Illinois in 1933 to acquire the Western Brewery in Belleville. Founded in 1851 by Philip Neu and Peter Gintz, the company became the Griesedieck Western Brewery Company, better known as "Stag," the brand name of the beer that it would produce. Griesedieck Western would continue as an independent until 1954, when it was acquired by Canada's Carling.

Up the Mississippi River in St. Paul, the Theodore Hamm Brewing Company greeted the Repeal of Prohibition with the engines of its delivery trucks already running at midnight on April 6, 1933. Two months later, however, near-disaster visited the Hamm family. The years of Prohibition had provided an open door for elements of organized crime, allowing men such as Al Capone to have a free reign in creating nefarious empires built on a foundation of illicit booze. One of the most notorious gangs of the gangster era was that of Arizona Donnie Clark Barker, best known simply as "Ma" Barker. By the 1920s, Ma's gang of bank robbers included her sons Herman, Lloyd, Arthur and Fred, among others. The Barker gang was also affiliated with the notorious Alvin Karpowicz, better known as "Creepy Karpis." In 1933, Ma Barker made a corporate decision to change the gang's direction from bank robbery to kidnapping for ransom.

On the afternoon of June 15, 1933, as was his habit, William Hamm, Jr. left the brewery offices on East Minnehaha Avenue and started walking toward the Hamm family mansion on Cable Avenue. Two blocks from his office door, Hamm was accosted by Creepy Karpis and Fred Barker, who shoved him into a car. He was taken to a house at Bensonville, Illinois, near Chicago. Demands were made that

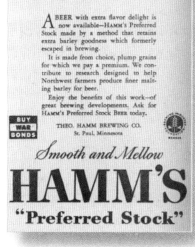

Above: Hamm's, Rainier and Mound City brewery ephemera from the 1940s. (*Collection of the author*)

Left: Rainier in the service of the troops. *Right:* The classic Lucky Lager die-cut label. *Below:* This Acme label was for low alcohol "Light" beer, but the highly-detailed artwork was used on most Acme labels through the 1940s. (*Collection of the author*) *Far right:* An Acme tap. (*Bill Yenne photo*) *Opposite:* US sailors enjoy their beer on Mog Mog Island in the South Pacific in 1944. (*National Archives*)

the Hamm family should pay $100,000 for his return. The payment was made, and three days later, William Hamm walked free. A Chicago bootlegger named Roger Touhy was later charged with the kidnapping, but he was acquitted. Ma and Fred Barker were killed by FBI agents in 1935, and Creepy Karpis was arrested on other charges. A one-time "Public Enemy Number One," Karpis would later have the distinction of being the longest serving resident of Alcatraz.

From Alcatraz, Karpis could see the lights of San Francisco, but not taste the city's signature beer. In the 1930s and 1940s, that beer was Acme. The brand was to the San Francisco Bay Area what the Rainier brand was to the Northwest. The brand actually dated to 1907 — the year after the Great San Francisco Earthquake — and opening of the Acme Brewing Company on Sansome Street, at the foot of Telegraph Hill. In 1916, four years before Prohibition, it was acquired by the California Brewing Association, which had evolved from the Glueck and Hansen National Brewery, started in 1861.

When the company resumed brewing Acme after Repeal, the brand struck a cord with consumers, and sales mushroomed. Much of this was in the Southern California, so the company responded by constructing a new brewery on 49th Street in Los Angeles. Opening for business in 1935, the Southern California operation would formally do business as the Acme Brewing Company, while the San Francisco activity would be known officially as Acme Breweries until 1943, when the California Brewing Association name was readopted. The Acme brand name would continue to be used on the products brewed at both locations.

Meanwhile, an important sister company had emerged as the key to Acme's success. The Bohemian Distributing Company was based on a partnership formed in June 1921 between an energetic young beverage salesman named Frank Vitale, and J.S. Foto, who operated a small retail beverage store in Los Angeles. A year later, the two partners purchased 50 cases of Acme near beer, and this initial transaction evolved into an association with the two Acme breweries that was the key to the brand becoming the de facto "national beer" of California.

Another great twentieth century brand that emerged from San Francisco was Lucky Lager, which was introduced by General Brewing Corporation in 1934. The beer, universally known as "Lucky," was so popular that the company would later rename itself as "Lucky Lager Brewing." Lucky Lager quickly became an important cultural fixture, promoting itself in everything from billboards near Seals Stadium, San Francisco's Pacific Coast League baseball park, to sponsorship of popular radio programs. One of the best remembered of the latter was "Lucky Lager Dance Time," a live music program that was aired on radio station KSFO in San Francisco in the years immediately following World War II.

Just THE KISS OF THE HOPS

You don't have to drink a bitter beer. Schlitz methods of brewing control capture *only* the delicate flavor of the hops, not their harsh bitterness. That's one reason for that famous flavor found only in Schlitz. Taste Schlitz and you'll never want to go back to a bitter beer.

At the time that the United States entered World War II in December 1941, the American brewing industry was just getting back on its feet after the twin body blows of Prohibition and the Depression. Naturally, there were a few cries for a replay of the situation in 1917 when it became the policy of the United States to discourage and restrict brewing and the consumption of beer. In fact, it was proposed that service personnel should not have access to beer and that areas surrounding military installations be rendered "dry." These cries fell on deaf ears.

The prohibitionist tendencies in popular culture that reached their frenzied crescendo during World War I had long since run their course. Beer was now seen as essential to the morale of the troops, as well as workers on the home front. To his credit, General George C. Marshall, Chief of Staff of the US Army went in exactly the *opposite* direction, readopting the notion of a beer ration for the troops which had been championed by George Washington

during the American Revolution. Access to beer with an alcohol content of 3.2 percent was permitted on military bases, and in July 1943, the United States government went so far as to require the brewing industry to set aside 15 percent of its production for the troops.

After having seen World War I as a catalyst for Prohibition, the situation was now reversed. The most critical problem faced by the United States brewing industry in World War II was how to get an adequate supply of beer to the troops overseas.

It was during World War II that the United States brewing industry climbed out of a slump that it had been in for nearly three decades. The peak of production during the 1930s was 58.8 million barrels in 1937, but this was below all but one of the years between 1910 and 1917 when the industry was at its zenith. Industry output did not top the 1937 numbers until it reached 63.7 million barrels in 1942. This was the third best year in history — behind 1913 and 1914.

In 1943, however, the annual output reached 71 million barrels, setting a new record. In 1944, the year that Americans finally realized that they were going to win the war, production mushroomed to 81 million barrels, and never looked back.

Below: Selling Schlitz in California's Acme country.
(*Collection of OnlyClassics.com*)

Chapter 5

NATIONAL BEERS
AND REGIONAL FAVORITES

MERICA HAD EMERGED FROM THE first world war into a dark decade of Prohibition, followed by another dark decade of Depression. However, the United States emerged from the horrors of World War II into an era of unprecedented prosperity. The expansive national mood of the 1950s and 1960s also saw a golden age of advertising as consumer products became barometers of prosperity. For beer and brewing, advertising was important not only for individual breweries, but for the industry as a whole. In 1949, the United States Brewers's Foundation launched institutional campaigns aimed at what Carl W. Badenhausen called "the need for getting a wider social acceptance of beer and ale." The two campaigns, based on the slogans "Beer Belongs" and "America's Beverage of Moderation," helped show that the enjoyment of beer was part of the evolving culture of America.

Nevertheless, beer sales in the United States seemed to have sought a level and remained more or less at that level through the 1950s. While sales every year from 1943 forward remained higher than at any time in history before the war, growth was essentially stagnant.

The annual output increased from 71 million barrels in 1943 to 81.7 million the following year — and reached 91.3 million in 1948 as wartime and postwar restrictions were lifted. However, during the 1950s, total production became stagnant, hovering around 89 million barrels annually until 1960.

During this period, two new trends began that would be hallmarks of the industry through much of the rest of the twentieth century. First, the gulf between a small number of big brewers and the rest of the industry, grew wider and wider. Second, multi-site brewing became a standard means for the big brewers to get bigger.

The biggest of the big were Anheuser-Busch and the two Milwaukee giants, Pabst and Schlitz. They were followed by the big New York brewers and Falstaff. Anheuser-Busch had surpassed two million barrels in 1938, and Pabst and Schlitz caught up in 1943. By this time, the *Brewers Journal* noted that Anheuser-Busch was pushing 3.5 million. After the war, the relative places would change as the big brewing companies raced to become true multi-site breweries. In 1950, Schlitz was the nation's largest brewing company with five million barrels of annual production, just slightly ahead of Anheuser-Busch. By 1960, the positions were reversed again, with Schlitz producing 5.6 million barrels against Anheuser-Busch's 8.5 million.

Schlitz had been early in recognizing the importance of distribution and multi-site brewing, and in fact the company had built a satellite brewery in Cleveland, Ohio from scratch in 1908 and had operated there for two years. In 1932, Pabst had acquired the small Premier Malt Products in Peoria Heights, Illinois, and had been operating that plant.

Though overshadowed by the larger firms after the war, Falstaff had actually been the true pioneer of large-scale, multi-site brewing, the first with a chain of breweries in three states. Beginning in 1934, Papa Joe Griesedieck and his son Alvin had expanded from their St. Louis base, buying larger breweries in New Orleans and Omaha. As Stanley Baron put it in his 1962 book *Brewed in America*, "This happened quite naturally in the history of Falstaff; it suited the market it had developed since its post-Repeal incorporation and was economically more advisable than buying land in St. Louis and adding to the existing capacity there."

Above: Thanksgiving dinner, circa the 1950s, with lager on the table. *Opposite:* Enjoying camaraderie and a glass of beer while waiting for the train. (*Collection of the author*)

Baron might also have said that the Griesedieck model was a template for what the larger brewing companies would do. They would use the Falstaff template, but they would not use the Falstaff map. Pabst, Schlitz and Anheuser-Busch were ready to truly go *national*, so the map was of the whole United States, not just its mid-section. They wanted a truly national system of satellite breweries on a scale unheard of prior to World War II. The obvious expansion would be into the large population centers on the two coasts — New York and California. The former was the largest, so the former was the first target market for expansion.

Pabst got into the New York market before either Schlitz or Anheuser-Busch, through the purchase of the Hoffman Beverage Company of Newark in 1946. Schlitz was next, when it bought the George Ehret Brewery in Brooklyn in 1949. Anheuser-Busch opted to build a brand new plant in Newark, New Jersey, which opened in 1951.

Falstaff reached toward the rapidly expanding California market itself by acquiring Wieland's Brewery in San Jose in 1952, making it the first major eastern brewer to expand into the Golden State, beating both Schlitz and Anheuser-Busch

(who were then concentrating on the New York area) by two years.

Between 1954 and 1956, Falstaff purchased breweries in Indiana and moved into Texas — again ahead of Anheuser-Busch and Schlitz — by opening breweries in El Paso and Galveston. Falstaff also moved deeper into California, briefly operating two breweries in San Francisco. The West Coast expansion was explained by a 48.5 percent population increase in California between 1950 and 1960. As the national breweries arrived in the Far West, a spontaneous cultural phenomenon quickly came into place in beer advertising. Menus in bars and restaurants also made widespread use of it. This phenomenon was the strict delineation between home-grown "Western Beer" and "Eastern Beer," the beer made by the interloping national brands.

In 1954, Schlitz and Anheuser-Busch became the first brewers with a coast-to-coast network of breweries, as they both opened new state-of-the-art facilities in the Los Angeles area. Schlitz, the postwar industry leader, then made its next move in 1956 by acquiring the former Muehlebach Brewery in Kansas City, Missouri — Anheuser-Busch's back yard. In 1959 both of these national giants opened facilities in Tampa, Florida, but by the following year, Anheuser-Busch had permanently replaced Schlitz as America's leading brewer.

After acquiring the Hoffman Beverage Company in 1946, Pabst's expansion was much slower than Schlitz and Anheuser-Busch. In 1958 Pabst bought the Blatz Brewery, one of its original Milwaukee rivals. From its small number of sites, Pabst had remained among the top five national brewers without expansion until 1972, when a new brewery was opened at Perry, Georgia, and 1979, when the company acquired the Blitz-Weinhard Brewery in Portland, Oregon.

Comparing the industry expansion of the 1950s to what had happened a half century earlier, Stanley Baron wrote "These moves were not like the consolidations and mergers that took place before the First World War. In those days it had not been considered feasible to manufacture the same brand in various parts of the country. For one thing, the label was associated with a particular location; and besides, the chemical processing of water to be used for brewing had not reached a sufficiently sophisticated stage to ensure identity of product. But in the years following the Second World War, when the operation of subsidiary plants in various parts of the country became common practice among the national brewers, the beer manufactured in California, the Midwest and New York, under one label, was sold as being identical in every respect."

Over the course of the next 16 years, Anheuser-Busch began brewing at six additional locations: Houston, Texas in 1966; Columbus, Ohio in 1968; Jacksonville, Florida in 1969; Merrimack, New Hampshire in 1970; Williamsburg, Virginia in 1972; at Fairfield, California near San Francisco in 1976; and at Baldwinsville, New York at a plant acquired from Schlitz in 1980.

Schlitz expanded into the South with new breweries at Longview, Texas in 1966; Winston-Salem, North Carolina in 1970; and Memphis, Tennessee in 1971. In 1963, Schlitz acquired the Burgermeister Brewing Company of San Francisco. Adding "Burgie" to the Schlitz portfolio would boost sales nearly 20 percent. Ironically, the Burgermeister facility, which was started in San Francisco in 1868, had been known as the "Milwaukee" Brewery from 1880 until Prohibition. Schlitz sold it to Meisterbrau of Chicago in 1969, and it would be part of the Falstaff portfolio from 1971 to 1978.

Above: **Hamm's is part of the fun at the 1950s patio party.** *Opposite:* **Papa bear raids the fridge for a midnight Schlitz.** (*Collection of the author*)

Another addition to the product line in 1963 was a high alcohol lager that would be known as Schlitz Malt Liquor. The term "malt liquor" was a legal requirement because of the high alcohol content of this particular lager. Contrary to the popular myth, there is no such style of beer as "malt liquor." The label of this new product pictured a bull that was actually based a photograph of Henry Uihlein's prize bull named "Prince."

While Schlitz continued to be marketed as the Beer That Made Milwaukee Famous, its advertising people toyed with a number of other secondary slogans. During the 1940s, when it was the largest selling brand in the United States, Schlitz had been consistently advertised as "America's most distinguished beer." During the 1960s, the term "Gusto" was worked into a number of print ads and television commercials. The phrase "When you're out of

Above and right: **The F. & M. Schaefer Brewery in Brooklyn was one of America's five largest in 1948.** (*Library of Congress*)

Schlitz, you're out of beer," was introduced in 1966 and used in both print and broadcast advertising.

In 1964, Schlitz moved farther west than any of its big rivals, acquiring the Hawaii Brewing Company, located on Kamehameha Highway in Honolulu. Founded just after Prohibition, the company's Primo Beer had developed a loyal cult following throughout the islands. Schlitz would continue brewing Primo in Hawaii until 1979, but attempts to keep up the mystique after production moved to the mainland would be unsuccessful.

In the decade between 1949 and 1958, according to the *Brewers' Almanac*, more than 185 brewers were forced either to close down or sell out. Of the top 52 breweries in 1942, 17 were absorbed by others, and four simply failed or stopped functioning. Of the 230 breweries in operation in 1961, only 40 were independently operated. In his commentary on this issue, Stanley Baron looked with nostalgia toward the earlier golden age of the American brewing industry a half century before, when he wrote "In the brewing industry, many of the plants that have gone entirely or been absorbed into one of the chains were poorly organized and lacking in a kind of dynamism which

brewers had to a great degree before the first World War."

Of course, the huge New York City brewers, notably Ballantine, Schaefer and Ruppert, were certainly big enough and powerful enough to have become national brewers if they had been so inclined. In 1950, Ballantine was number three nationally, and Schaefer was number five. However, it was probably for the reason of size that they did not go national.

Maybe it was, to paraphrase Stanley Baron, simply a lack of dynamism. Why should they expend their energy on national expansion when they were sitting on top of the hemisphere's largest beer market? They felt that they could remain as regional brewers and still be among the biggest nationally.

Schaefer did operate satellite breweries east of the Mississippi in Albany, New York (1950-1972), Cleveland, Ohio (1961-1963) and Baltimore, Maryland (1963-1978) to help meet the demand for his popular brew. In 1972, when the Albany facility was closed, its production was transferred to a new, ultramodern brewery near Allentown in Pennsylvania's Lehigh Valley. In 1976 Schaefer's 60-year-old Brooklyn brewery, no longer economically viable, was closed. Four years

Above: **Relaxing with a schooner of Schlitz.** (*Bill Yenne photo*)

later, Schaefer became merely a brand name of Stroh and Allentown became a Stroh facility.

Ballantine sort of became a "multi-site brewery" in 1943, when it bought what was literally "the brewery next door." Also located on Newark's Freeman Street, this brewery dated from the one founded on the site in 1866 by Charles Kolb. It had become the Christian Feigenspan Brewery in 1875 and had been famous during the 1930s for its Munich and Pride of Newark brands. This facility would operate as Ballantine Plant Two until 1948, when it was closed permanently.

Nevertheless, Ballantine continued to grow. By 1950, the company had an annual output of 4.4 million barrels and was the third largest brewing company in the United States, behind Anheuser-Busch and Schlitz. Its products now included both the long standing India Pale Ale and the Ballantine XXX lager. Perhaps more significant than the national standing was that Ballantine was now number one in the New York City area. This was underscored by the fact that Ballantine was now the beer that sponsored the New York Yankees — the baseball team that rival brewery tycoon Jacob Rup-

Above: Toasting Valentine's Day with a glass of Ballantine. *Right*: A young man shares a cold bottle of Blatz with his appreciative date. (*Collection of the author*)

pert had owned until his death in 1939. Throughout the 1940s and 1950s, the legendary Yankees radio announcer Mel Allen, would refer to home runs hit at Yankee Stadium as "Ballantine Blasts." Ruppert had to have been rolling over in his grave.

Ballantine had become such a part of life in America's media capital that even literary figures found it natural to mention the brand. Frank Sinatra mentioned it on stage and John Steinbeck alluded to Ballantine in prose. "I would rather have a bottle of Ballantine Ale than any other drink after fighting a really big fish," wrote Ernest Hemingway in a rare product endorsement. "We keep it iced in the bait box with chunks of ice packed around it. And you ought to taste it on a hot day when you have worked a big marlin fast because there were sharks after him."

For Ballantine itself, there were sharks in the water. These sharks were the sharks of changing times and changing tastes. These were also the times of the national brands, times with which Ballantine had failed to keep pace. Ballantine closed its Newark brewery in 1971 and was reduced to simply a brand name.

Even as Ballantine and Schaefer were hanging on to market share in the New York metropolitan area in the 1950s, another brewer was competing for the share of publicity that the city gave its local brewers. The history of beer marketing is filled with unforgettable slogans and extraordinary campaigns, but that which was used between 1940 and 1965 to market the Rheingold brand captured the imagination of its target audience like no other. The "Miss Rheingold" campaign was literally the talk of the town in America's largest metropolitan area for a quarter of a century. When the Liebmann Breweries of Brooklyn nominated its six candidates for each annual Miss Rheingold title, the enthusiasm for the election campaign rivaled that of a presidential election.

In 1939, Philip Liebmann, the grandson of the brewery's founder, and Bob Wechsler, who worked for the point of sale advertising and promotion agency that handled the Rheingold account, came up with the idea to have a "Miss Rheingold" represent the company in advertising. A young Spanish-born Chilean actress and model named Eugenia Lincoln Falkenburg — best known by her nickname, "Jinx," — reigned as the first "Rheingold Girl" in 1940. Her face appeared on point of purchase materials as well as on packaging and in newspaper

Above: This cowboy appreciates the "three rings" of quality originally articulated by Peter Ballantine in 1879. (*Collection of the author*)

and magazine advertising. As "Rheingold Girl" for 1941, Liebmann selected a young model named Ruth Ownbey.

The following year, it was decided that the Rheingold Girl should be voted upon by Rheingold consumers from a panel of six, and that she should be known as "Miss Rheingold." The customers decided, and young Nancy Drake became the first Miss Rheingold chosen by popular vote.

The same process would continue for more than two decades. Miss Rheingold and the annual election would become a major phenomenon in the five boroughs and beyond. Her face was everywhere from publicity events to cartoons in *The New Yorker*. By the late 1940s, the number of votes reached into the millions. During the 1950s, the count exceeded 15 million annually, more than the votes cast

Above: Miss Rheingold candidates visit Republic Aviation in Farmingdale, Long Island. Madelyn Darrow won in 1958, Robin Bain in 1959. *Right:* Sonia Gover, Miss Rheingold of 1943. *Opposite:* Hillie Merrit. (*Collection of the author*)

in general elections. In 1952, 25 million votes were cast in the election that made Mary Austin the Miss Rheingold of 1953. This was about a dozen times the number of votes cast in New York City that year for Dwight Eisenhower and Adlai Stevenson, the major candidates in the presidential election.

The selection process that picked the half dozen finalists each year would receive as much press attention as the Miss America contest. Held for many years at New York City's glamorous Waldorf Astoria Hotel, the lavish program featured celebrity judges that included movie stars from Douglas Fairbanks Jr. to Joan Fontaine. Though many women competed in the annual event at the Waldorf, only six were chosen for the final round of public voting. The rest went home discouraged. In 1948, one such 19-year-old, rejected from the final six, boarded the train for Philadelphia determined not to let it keep her down. Like many young ladies of her age, she had big dreams. Turned down by Rheingold, she decided to try Hollywood. It was a good thing she didn't give up. Her name was Grace Kelly.

Most of the Miss Rheingolds and their runners up melted back into rela-

tive obscurity after their year of fame. However, several continued in show business and a few achieved stardom. Jinx Falkenburg went on to appear in a total of more than a dozen feature films. Emily Banks, Miss Rheingold of 1960, had a career in television. Carol Merrill, a runner-up for Miss Rheingold of 1963, was a regular on the television game show "Let's Make a Deal." Two other runners-up who had especially important screen careers were Hope Lange and Nathalie "Tippi" Hedren, who became one of Alfred Hitchcock's favorite leading ladies. Celeste Yarnall, Miss Rheingold of 1964, would be the last of the lineage chosen by popular balloting in the twentieth century. She went on to a successful Hollywood career. Having appeared with Paul Newman in *A New Kind of Love* (1963), she had the title

"My beer is *Rheingold* —the *Dry* beer!"

says HILLIE MERRITT
MISS RHEINGOLD 1956

"The new ACME can looks wonderful

ACME
LIGHT DRY BEER
NET CONTENTS 12 FLUID OUNCES

...and just wait 'til you taste the beer!"

Above: To update its image, Acme Brewing introduced a new can design in 1950 amid great fanfare. The design mimicked the appearance of beer in a glass. *(Acme collection, North Coast Brewing Company)*
Right: Cowboys and Western movies were cultural icons in the 1950s, but Lucky also used him to underscore its identity as a "Western" beer. *(Collection of the author)*
Opposite: Beer was part of entertaining "out west." *(Collection of the author)*

role in the cult classic *The Face of Eve* (1968) and she starred opposite Elvis Presley in *Live a Little, Love a Little* (1968). The last of the dynasty would be Sharon Vaughn, Miss Rheingold of 1965, selected by acclamation, the choice of brewery executives.

In the meantime, Philip Liebmann would take a run at making Rheingold the only one of the big New York City brewing companies to operate breweries in the West. In 1954, he boldly reached coast-to-coast to purchase the former Acme breweries in Los Angeles and San Francisco. However, this costly venture would be terminated after just four years.

Out west, Acme had emerged from World War II still wearing the unofficial mantle of the national beer of California. When the United States entered the war, Acme became a leading supplier of beer to troops operating in the Pacific Theater. To meet wartime demand, the breweries in San Francisco and Los Angeles both underwent major upgrades. The new Acme Brewery in Los Angeles was dedicated in June 1943. In San Francisco, Acme's expansion plans included construction of a new brewing plant near the site of the old National Brewery in San Francisco. Architects described this new edifice as "one of the world's most beautiful industrial buildings."

After the war, the California economy emerged as the largest and perhaps the most robust in the nation. As the 1950s began, the entire country was in the midst of an economic boom that was unprecedented in world history. Against this backdrop, Acme flourished. The 1950s promised great things for consumer products companies. The expanding economy made the road ahead look like clear sailing. However, regional brewers everywhere needed to keep an eye on their rear-view mirrors. The national breweries, which had hardly been a factor before World War II, were gaining, and gaining faster than anyone imagined.

Until the 1950s, brands such as Acme and Lucky Lager owned the California market, but the national giants now smelled money in the exploding California economy. Falstaff went into Northern California in 1952, with a brewery acquisition in San Jose, and Pabst arrived in 1953, acquiring the Eastside Brewery on North Main Street in Los Angeles. As noted earlier, both Anheuser-Busch and Schlitz went into Acme's back yard — the rapidly growing San Fernando Valley, immediately north of the city of Los Angeles — in 1954.

That same year, Acme sold the two breweries to Liebmann. In 1958, the nearly new San Francisco brewery, which had been heralded in 1942 as an architectural beauty, was simply closed. The Los Angeles brewery would be sold to Hamm's and

operated until 1972. The Acme brand was brewed by Blitz-Weinhard of Portland, Oregon through the 1970s.

Despite the moves by Anheuser-Busch and Schlitz into Southern California, the Western regionals — except Acme — fared better during the quarter century after World War II than their counterparts in the Northeast.

As Acme's star dimmed, Lucky Lager emerged as a leading "Western Beer," expanding during the 1950s and 1960s from its California roots to the entire West. The brand's signature, double entendre, slogan, "It's Lucky When You Live in California," was changed to read "It's Lucky When You Live in America." At its peak, Lucky Lager — which frequently changed its corporate name back and forth to and from General Brewing Corporation — had breweries spread over a larger area than any company other than the coast-to-coast national brands. It all began in 1950 with the acquisition of the Interstate Brewing Company in Vancouver, Washington, directly across the Columbia River from Portland, Oregon. The aptly named Interstate would be the springboard to Lucky Lager's major market penetration into the Northwest and the intermountain West, especially

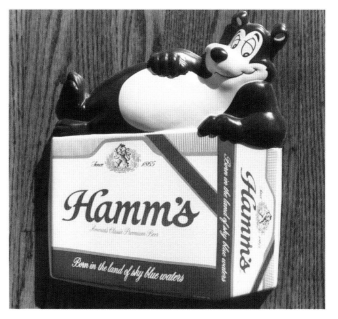

Washington, Oregon and Montana. Next came the acquisition of the Fisher Brewing Company in Salt Lake City.

The Theodore Hamm Brewing Company of St. Paul was, like Lucky, essentially a regional company that was a major competitor to the national brands from the 1950s through the 1960s. William C. Figge, son of former Hamm's brewmaster William Figge, left his law career to become president of the Theodore Hamm Brewing Company in 1951.

The expanding postwar American economy afforded numerous opportunities for growing a business, and Figge decided to seize the moment and transform Hamm's from a regional favorite into a national brand to be reckoned with. Working with Ray Mithun of the Campbell-Mithun advertising agency, he oversaw the development of the immortal slogan, "From the Land of Sky Blue Waters." The notion that Minnesota was a recreation paradise of "10,000 Lakes" was already being promoted, and the two slogans neatly supported one another. Indeed, the state would later honor Figge by naming a lake in the Superior National Forest after him.

Campbell-Mithun next moved to create characters to inhabit it. Nobody really recalls for sure who came up with the idea of an animated bear to promote Hamm's Beer. Albert Whitman at Campbell-Mithun is believed to have been the first to suggest a menagerie of small animals to inhabit the mythical "Land of Sky Blue Waters." The Los Angeles animation firm of Swift-Chaplin did most of the film animation featuring the bear, and, because Howard Swift had created animals for Disney animated features in the 1940s, it is suggested that he may have originated the bear. However, the bear was most probably created by Cleo Hovel, an

Above and far right: **The Hamm's Bear is one of the most beloved spokesmodels in the history of beer advertising.** *Right:* **In the 1950s, Hamm's advertising also highlighted beautifully airbrushed illustrations of lager glasses.** (*Collection of the author*)

illustrator and creative director at Campbell-Mithun, who ultimately did many of the drawings used in print advertising.

Hamm's turned to the big new media of the early 1950s — television. Advertising agencies were swift to embrace it and the "television commercial" was born. The notion of using animated characters in television advertising was soon adopted. Among the first to use it for pitching beer was the Piel Brothers Brewing Company in New York City. They had crafted two lovable characters Bert and Harry, who utilized the voiceovers of the comedy team of Bob Elliot and Ray Goulding. Meanwhile, the Jackson Brewery in New Orleans, brewers of Jax Beer, created the "Elephant and Bartender" characters in the late 1950s and early 1960s that were voiced by Mike Nichols and Elaine May.

As popular as the others were, none approached the broad popularity of the Hamm's Bear. He made his television debut in 1953, and evolved into one of the most recognized imaginary animals in advertising history. Joined by a fox, a beaver, squirrels and other creatures, he starred in countless commercials, engaged in some outdoor activity against the backdrop of the drumming "From the Land of

Sky Blue Waters" jingle orchestrated by Ernie Gavin of radio station WCCO.

During the 1950s and 1960s, the Hamm's Bear was also adapted for print advertising and point of purchase items, winning numerous advertising awards for Campbell-Mithun, and helping push sales of Hamm's beer. Another popular point of purchase item used by Hamm's during this period were the full-color lighted motion signs. Manufactured for use in bars and taverns, they had a moving scroll with images of campfire, waterfalls and canoes on the shore of a lake, set against north woods backdrop. Today, such signs still fetch hundreds of dollars on the collectibles market.

Between 1951 and 1954, Hamm's moved from fifteenth place among American breweries, with a 1.2 million barrel annual output, to eighth place with 2.3 million barrels. Distribution spread beyond Minnesota to encompass 30 states, plus the Territory of Alaska. To keep pace with demand, Figge set out to acquire other breweries outside of Minnesota and turn them into Hamm's breweries. In 1953, he bought the former Rainier Brewing Company facility near Seals' Stadium in San Francisco. Five years later, in 1958, he bought the former Acme Brewery on 49th

Above: **The end of a day of fishing in "the land of sky blue waters."** (*Collection of the author*)

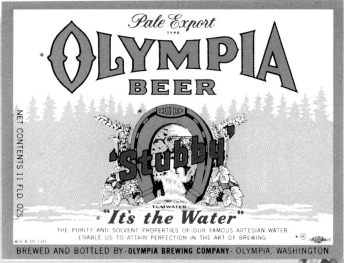

Street in Los Angeles. In 1959, he acquired the Gunther Brewing Company in Baltimore.

However, this experience was not so good. Resentment over the demise of Gunther as a brand, combined with bad publicity over a batch of beer that was allowed to freeze, made the Baltimore venture a failure. After an attempt was made

to revive the Gunther brand, the brewery was sold off to Schaefer in 1963. That same year, however, Hamm's bought the Gulf Brewing Company, that had been started in Houston, Texas in 1933.

The annual output at Hamm's reached 3.8 million barrels by 1964 and peaked at 4.3 million four years later. In 1965, as the Hamm Brewing Company

Above: The 11-ounce, short-necked "Stubby" bottle was the signature packaging for "Oly." The horseshoe and Tumwater Falls were the trademark widely recognized throughout the West. *Right:* An Olympia delivery truck making its rounds. (*Collection of the author*)

celebrated its centennial, the company was put up for sale. Both Molson in Canada and Rheingold expressed interest in buying it, but their acquisitions were barred by the United States Justice Department on antitrust grounds. Hamm's was considered too big to be acquired by a brewing company. The winning bid of $10.4 million came for hard liquor holding company Heublein. The acquisition was approved, and William Figge retired in 1966 at the age of 61.

The Pacific Northwest was home to three prominent regionals who rivaled both the nationals and the super-regionals like Lucky Lager through the 1960s and into the 1970s. These were the Blitz-Weinhard Brewery in Portland, Olympia in Tumwater, Washington, and Emil Sick's Rainier brand in Seattle. Olympia was marketed in California and exported to the Pacific rim. So widespread was the brand's impact in the western United States that by the 1960s, "Oly" was being referred to as the "national beer of Montana," even though it was an out-of-state brand and Montana had important commercial breweries within the state until nearly the end of the decade. It was hard to find a tavern in the Northwest or Mountain West that didn't have an illu-

minated Oly "Waterfall and Horseshoe" trademark sign, and few supermarkets in the West did not stock six-packs of the familiar short-necked, brown Olympia bottles known as "stubbies."

Oly also had a tremendous presence in California as home-grown brands such as Acme faded. Indeed, Olympia would have a 24 percent market share in the Golden State during the 1960s. Between 1963 and the peak year of 1974, production at the Tumwater brewery increased from two million barrels to 4.3 million barrels annually.

At Rainier in Seattle, meanwhile, Emil Sick had been gradually divesting himself of his brewing interests. In 1956, he sold a majority interest in Sick's Seattle Brewing & Malting to Molson Breweries, Ltd., Canada's oldest and largest brewing concern. In turn, the Seattle-based entity came to be known as Sick's Rainier Brewing Company. Over the next decade, the former Sick empire would gradually be disassembled. The Sick name would be officially dropped from the corporate appellation in 1970.

Sick's Lethbridge Brewery was sold outright to Molson Western Breweries Ltd. in 1959. It would survive for three decades until it was shuttered after the merger of Molson with Carling O'Keefe.

Right: A label from Emil Sick's Rainier Brewery in Spokane.
(Collection of the author)
Below: A big rig pulls in to load at Sick's Highlander Brewery in Missoula, Montana, circa 1960. *(Courtesy of Ron Beierle)*

When Emil Sick passed away in 1964, his Canadian brewery and his Seattle baseball team were gone and his breweries in the United States were slipping away. The Salem brewery had ceased production in 1953, but the others would continue until the 1960s, when the Sick's Breweries would be heavily impacted by the market penetration of the national mega-brewers and the general consolidation within the industry. The Spokane brewery was closed in 1962, and the Highlander facility in Missoula followed in 1964 — although the Highlander brand would continue to be brewed in Seattle.

By 1960, the fourth largest brewing company in the United States was actually Canadian. Carling was also then Canada's third largest brewery. Several decades before the deal with Sick, Carling had made its first inroads in the United States through the Brewing Corporation of America in Cleveland, Ohio. In 1954, the name was changed to Carling Brewing Company, and the following year this entity acquired the former Griesedieck West-ern breweries in Belleville, Illinois and St. Louis — famous for the Stag brand. This was the company owned by Henry Griesedieck, the cousin to the Falstaff Griesediecks.

In 1956 Carling added additional breweries in Natick, Massachusetts and Frankenmuth, near Detroit. Two years later the Canadian-based brewer put out its shingle in Atlanta, Georgia and Tacoma, Washington, creating an archipelago of breweries that was the envy of many American brewers.

During the early 1960s Carling opened breweries in Baltimore, Fort Worth and Phoenix, but the latter part of the decade was marked by the company's gradual decline in the market. Business declined in the ensuing decade, and in 1979 Carling (Carling O'Keefe after 1973) left the United States market, selling off its holdings to American companies. In 1989, Carling O'Keefe was absorbed by Molson, creating a merged entity that was Canada's largest brewing company.

It retrospect, it seems inevitable that the 1960s would see a widespread brewing industry consolidation. The power of eastern beer would heavily impact the westerners. A generation later a renaissance would sweep the West, as craft brewers managed to outmaneuver the national brands with superior quality, but in the 1960s, the regionals erroneously believed that they had to compete on price. Ultimately it would be their undoing.

The total volume of beer being produced in the United States increased slightly from 88.8 million barrels in 1950 to 94.5 million in 1960, but the market share of the top ten brewing companies increased from 38 to 52 percent. For the top five, it increased from 24 to 32 percent. In 1960, Anheuser-Busch had an annual output of 8.5 million barrels compared to 5.7 million for Schlitz and 4.9 million for third-place Falstaff. Together, the three industry leaders had cornered nearly a quarter of the American beer market. The age of the great and powerful national brewers had arrived. By 1970, annual volume was up to 134.7 million barrels, with the top ten controlling 69 percent and half of annual production concentrated with the top five. During the 1970s, annual output soared to 188.4 million barrels, but by now the top ten accounted for 93 per-

cent, with the top five having a 75 percent share.

Anheuser-Busch emerged as the market leader and extended its lead by building new facilities rather than by acquiring existing breweries. Elsewhere, mergers and acquisitions defined the industry. One of the most auspicious was the acquisition of Milwaukee's Miller Brewing by the Philip Morris tobacco company. Philip Morris bought a 53 percent share from the W.R. Grace Company in 1969 and the remaining shares in 1970. Within a decade, Miller had risen from number seven to number two nationally.

In the 1970s, after two decades of expansion and acquisition, brewing companies moved in to shed breweries as fast as they had been acquired. For Heublein-owned Hamm's, the first property to be divested was the former Gulf Brewing site in Houston, which was simply closed in 1967 after four years of operation. The Los Angeles brewery was closed in 1972. The giant San Francisco brewery was used by Heublein between 1969 and 1973 to brew the Burgermeister ("Burgie") product. By now, as sales had begun to slip, Heublein was anxious to divest the entire company. In 1973, a group of seven Hamm's distributors organized under the name Brewers

Right: **The products of Canada's Carling, including Red Cap, were brewed in Cleveland until 1971.** *Below:* **Ireland's Arthur Guinness, Sons & Company brewed their legendary Extra Stout on Long Island from 1948 to 1954.** (*Collection of the author*) *Opposite:* **Paintings from the US Brewers Foundation "Beer Belongs" series. The point is well taken. It *still* belongs!** (*Collection of the author*)

Here are Carling's two new throw-away bottles. Each contains 12 full ounces.

Unlimited to save the Hamm's name. They operated the San Francisco brewery until 1975, when it was closed permanently. In 1975, the Olympia Brewing Company of Tumwater, Washington paid $14.7 million for Hamm's. Eight years later, Olympia was, itself, acquired by the Pabst Brewing Company of Milwaukee.

As the mega-brewers increased market share, once great regional brands began behaving like rudderless ships. Existing breweries were sold, new breweries bought and sold, and names changed and changed back. For example, one needs a scorecard to keep track of the corporate meanderings of Lucky Lager, aka General Brewing, during this period. To save money, General did what companies often are forced to do. It divested property. The Azusa site was sold to Miller Brewing in 1966, and the Salt Lake City plant was simply closed in 1967. Two years later, the two surviving General Brewing Corporation sites were renamed again for the brand name, although they were clearly owned by General.

Above: Some of the famous brands that were collected under the umbrella of Paul Kalmanovitz included 102, Falstaff, Narragansett and Ballantine. *(Collection of the author)*

Above: The stylized "L" logotype was used in Lucky Lager packaging late in its life as one of the West's great beers. *(Bill Yenne photo)*
Opposite: Both Hamm's and Pabst also became part of the Kalmanovitz holdings. *(Collection of the author)*

In 1971, still operating as Lucky Breweries, Inc., General Brewing acquired two additional plants as General breweries in the same general geographic regions as those that had been divested in 1966-1967.

The "new" General breweries were the former Maier Brewing Company in Los Angeles and the former Walter Brewing Company in Pueblo, Colorado. The latter traced its history back to the company started by Carl Roth in 1889. It would be officially named as the General Brewing Company of Colorado, but it would do business under the Walter Brewing Company name. These two 1971 acquisitions were simply closed in 1974 and 1975 respectively.

By way of the General meanderings, the name of the enigmatic Paul Kalmanovitz enters prominently into the story of the consolidation of regional brewers in the 1970s. A Polish immigrant entrepreneur, he bought the 102 Brewery in Los Angeles in 1950, and spent the next two decades fending off hostile takeover bids from Falstaff. In 1970 Kalmanovitz acquired the much larger General Brewing, merged it with his 102 Brewery and set up S&P Corporation as its parent. However, he hadn't forgotten Falstaff.

Above: A classic postwar holiday celebration with Pabst. (*Collection of the author*)

The reclusive and rarely seen Kalmanovitz would soon forge a substantial reputation within the industry. It was not that of a builder and dreamer in the mold of Frederick Pabst or Papa Joe Griesedieck, but as a consolidator and dismantler. In 1975, through his S&P Holdings company, he acquired his old rival, Falstaff and began a program of drastic downsizing. He quickly closed Falstaff's St. Louis headquarters and laid off hundreds of workers. He then moved to shutter Falstaff facilities just as fast as Alvin Griesedieck had added them two decades before.

In the meantime, Falstaff had acquired Ballantine in 1972 and the Narragansett Brewing Company in 1965. Narragansett, in Cranston, Rhode Island, had been established in 1890 and had become a popular brand name in New England. For this reason, Falstaff for a time continued operations under the Narragansett name.

One by one, the lights would go out on the great archipelago of Falstaff breweries built by Alvin and Papa Joe. The last Falstaff St. Louis plant — ironically the Griesedieck Brothers facility — closed in 1977. Falstaff's recently acquired San Francisco Brewery was shut down in 1978, followed in 1979 by the New Orleans facility, which had been a Falstaff Brewery for 40 years. Galveston was closed in 1981, and Omaha, Papa Joe's first out-of-state acquisition, was closed in 1987. The Narragansett Brewery was gone by 1984.

As for General Brewing, Kalmanovitz closed all of the breweries except the relatively new facility in Vancouver, Washington. It continued to operate until 1985, when he closed and dismantled the entire plant and shipped it to China, where it was reassembled at Zhouging. In 1985, he acquired Pabst, and along with it, the Olympia and Hamm's brand names. He promptly closed the Pabst flagship brewery in Milwaukee, but the Oly brewery at Tumwater, Washington was so modern and so efficient that it was indispensable.

The consolidation period saw the total

annual output of the industry double, even as the number of brewing companies shriveled from over 400 in 1950 to just 140 independent brewing companies in the early 1960s. There would be fewer than 50 as the 1980s began. As in many other industries, market share was concentrated more and more in the hands of fewer and fewer companies.

Schlitz, the previous number two brewing company, had maintained that position for a quarter century, while continuing to grow and to outpace a succession of third-place American brewers though the 1960s and early 1970s. However, the fortunes of Milwaukee's leading company began to sink in the 1970s after it reformulated its already pale lager to be even lighter. Schlitz was able to cut production costs, but the public perception was that Schlitz was also cutting the quality of the beer. Even as the company was investing in a nationwide plant expansion program, sales were declining.

The catalyst for the final downfall of Schlitz Brewing came in 1976, when millions of bottles of beer produced at the Memphis and Tampa breweries were determined to have gone bad. The image of these being destroyed was a public relations disaster.

An event symbolic of the times for Schlitz came in 1979, with the sale of its two-year-old Baldwinsville brewery to rival Anheuser-Busch. By 1981, Schlitz was on the ropes and entertaining buyout offers from Pabst and Heileman. The latter won the bidding, but the deal was nixed by the United States Justice Department on anti-trust grounds. A year later, the Stroh Brewing Company of Detroit made an offer that pleased the feds. In March 1982, the brewer that brewed the beer that had made Milwaukee famous was sold to a brewer from Detroit, who would close the Schlitz plant in Milwaukee. In a further twist of irony, Stroh would close its own Detroit flagship brewery in 1985 to concentrate production at the former Schlitz facilities, notably at Winston-Salem and Tampa.

In the 1970s, the era of Paul Kalmanovitz and the Schlitz debacle, it was hard to find what Stanley Baron would have called the "kind of dynamism which brewers had to a great degree before the first World War." One company that did not lack dynamism during this period was San Antonio's Lone Star. Started by Adolphus Busch in 1884, the brewery reopened after Prohibition under a succession of owners before being taken over in

Above: During the 1940s and 1950s, Pabst celebrated a golden age of greatness as one of America's true national brands. This huge, lighted sign was erected above the Illinois Central Railroad tracks near the South Water Street freight depot in Chicago. (*Library of Congress*) Opposite: Beer is part of the fun at this living room jam session. These paintings were part of the "Beer Belongs" series from the US Brewers Foundation. (*Collection of the author*)

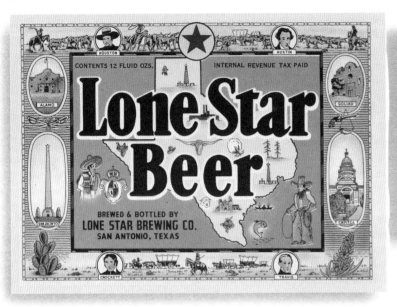

Above: During the middle part of the twentieth century, the Lone Star label was an amazing pictogram of Texas landmarks and milestones. During the "National Beer of Texas" days of the 1970s, the design was simplified considerably. *Right:* Twenty-first century packaging still prominently features the star motif. Lone Star has a long heritage of promoting Texas music. *(Collection of the author)*
Opposite: The classic Heileman can featured in this 1980s homage to legendary landscape painter Albert Bierstadt. *(Collection of the author)*

1940 by the George Muehlebach Brewing Company of Kansas City, Missouri — which had links to the Griesedieck Western Brewery of Belleville, Illinois, the brewers of the well-known Stag brand. Though the Muehlebach interests divested themselves of the brewery in 1949, the Lone Star name remained and the brewery evolved as an important fixture in San Antonio and Texas. In 1954, a distribution arrangement with Schroeder Distributing took Lone Star statewide. Newspaper ads proudly announced that "The beer I go for is goin' places. . . Clear across Texas!"

In the 1970s, Lone Star was reinvented and marketed as the "National Beer of Texas," and as the "official beer" of the "Outlaw Movement" in country music. Indeed, these two Texas cultural phenomena were inextricably intertwined in the 1970s. The Out-law Movement was essentially a reaction to mainstream country music, which had, by the late 1960s, become smooth and schmaltzy. Indeed, most of the music originating from Nashville at that time had more in common with mainstream pop music than with the genre pioneered by the likes of Hank Williams and Ernest Tubb a generation before. The Outlaw Movement sought to create a genre that relied more on rockabilly-style lead guitar than lush string sections. It was more of the type of music that one would expect in a honky tonk bar — and it was performed by people wearing jeans and cowboy boots rather than suits and ties. The leading exponents of the movement had roots in Texas. These included singers and songwriters such as Willie Nelson, Waylon Jennings, Jerry Jeff Walker, Billy Joe Shaver and David Allen Coe.

Lone Star Beer played a prominent role in the movement by sponsoring concerts and by positioning its advertising in conjunction with anything related to the Outlaw music and the personality cults of the Texas-based outlaws. Willie Nelson's annual Fourth of July "picnics," which were actually enormous outdoor concerts, were sponsored by the "National Beer of Texas." Lone Star even found its way into the lyrics of country songs. Red Steagall's 1976 song, "Lone Star Beer and Bob Wills Music," which was recorded by David Allan Coe, featured the line "Tell all the ladies I'm single, tell Lone Star Beer that I'm dry."

A significant anthem of the Outlaw Movement was the song "Mamas, Don't Let Your Babies Grow Up to be Cowboys," written by Ed and Patsy Bruce, and immortalized by Willie Nelson. It paid tribute to a pair of San Antonio-made commercial products that were essential elements of the Texas/Outlaw ethos with the line "Lone Star belt buckles and old faded Levi's, and each night begins a new day."

Just as Lone Star was beginning its new day as the National Beer of Texas, it ceased to be Texas-owned! Beginning in 1976, it would be sold, resold and owned by a succession of out of state companies including Washington's Olympia, Wisconsin's Heileman, Michigan's Stroh, and finally Pabst.

The story of Heileman is an interesting and unique tale from the era of brewery consolidations. The G. Heileman Brewing Company of LaCrosse, Wisconsin was a small regional brewer that grew to national prominence, not through the vehicle of a single national brand like Anheuser-Busch or Schlitz, but through assembling an amazing amalgam of important, formerly independent, regional brands — which would continue to operate under their original names. Heileman had specifically acquired the *signature* regional brewing companies in a number of important regions. Indeed, Heileman's own house brand, Heileman Old Style, had a wide regional following — especially in Chicago. In 1960, Heileman was the thirty-first largest brewer in the United States, but by 1982 it was fourth. One of its first major acquisitions had been that of Blatz — one of the big four names in Milwaukee — from Pabst in 1969. In 1986, while reviving the Blatz name, Heileman went to the unusual length of creating a short-lived, retro-style microbrewery in Milwaukee to brew the beer and market it against the backdrop of Milwaukee brewery nostalgia.

In 1976, Heileman bought the Grain Belt brand of Minneapolis and later acquired Jacob Schmidt Brewing from across the river in St. Paul and consolidated their operations. (In 1991, Heileman would sell the Grain Belt name and the Schmidt St. Paul brewery to the Minnesota Brewing Company.) In 1979, Heileman acquired four former Carling National

Right: During its apogee in the 1980s, the collection of brands owned and brewed by the G. Heileman Brewing Company of LaCrosse, Wisconsin was a veritable "who's who" of classic regional brands. They ranged from Schmidt, Stag and Falls City in the Midwest to Rainier and Henry Weinhard's in the Northwest. They ranged from the "National Beer of Texas" to the "Beer of Danish Kings," brewed under license fro Tuborg in Denmark. (*Collection of the author*) *Opposite:* Stoney's from Jones Brewing in Pennsylvania and Deer Brand from Minnesota's August Schell remained as independent brands through the end of the century. (*Courtesy of the breweries*) The 1960s illustration shows people happily enjoying lager at their picnic. (*Collection of the author*)

breweries in the United States from the Canadian brewing giant, including the former Griesedieck Western breweries in Belleville, Illinois and St. Louis. Along with the acquisition, Heileman picked up Griesedieck's popular Stag brand and a license to brew Carling's Black Label and Red Cap Ale.

During the early 1980s, Heileman went west to acquire Rainier, which Emil Sick had made into the signature beer of Seattle, as well as Portland's popular Blitz-Weinhard Company. In 1983, Heileman bought the Lone Star Brewing Company from Olympia. In 1987, Heileman itself was acquired by Alan Bond of Australia, whose holdings then constituted one of the world's largest multinational brewing companies, including Australia's Swan Brewery and the Pittsburgh Brewing Company, which brewed Iron City, the signature brand of western Pennsylvania.

Meanwhile, smaller consolidations also formed local conglomerates. A case in point was in Cincinnati, where Hudepohl and Schoenling merged in 1988 to form Hudepohl-Schoenling, which operated under the slogan — if not the official name — of "Cincinnati's Brewery." In the mid-1990s, Jim Koch of Boston Beer Company — a Cincinnati native —

purchased the Hudepohl-Schoenling Brewery as brewing location for the Samuel Adams brand.

Of course, not all of America's small independent regional breweries closed or were swallowed by the consolidation period of the 1970s and early 1980s. Several notable long-lived regional brewers survived to reach the turn of the century as vibrant and vital companies with both good beer and large numbers of loyal fans. Among these were Stevens Point, founded in 1857 in the Wisconsin city of the same name; August Schell of New Ulm, Minnesota, founded in 1860; Yuengling of Pottsville, Pennsylvania, founded in 1829 and the oldest brewing company in the United States; and Jones Brewing of Smithton, Pennsylvania.

The latter company was established in 1907 by Welsh immigrant William B. "Stoney" Jones in 1907 as the Eureka Brewing Company. The brewery's original brand was Eureka Gold Crown, but because Stoney Jones habitually made personal sales calls to taverns in the area, it came to be known unofficially as "Stoney's Beer." The brewery lost little time changing the official name. Until it finally closed in 2001, the company subscribed to the notion that "The beer most in demand is a

Left: A classic Wisconsin independent, Leinenkugel's retains its identity even after its 1987 acquisition by Miller Brewing. *Below:* Part of the Miller Brewing glassware collection. *Right:* toasting the day with a golden lager! *(Collection of the author)*

product brewed in the traditional fashion [and] that this is why foreign or imported beers are gaining an increasing share of the market. . . as Americans become more and more disenchanted with American 'fad' beers. The Jones Brewing Company, therefore, has chosen not to get involved in fads and gadgets, but instead will brew the finest natural (or traditional) beer possible!" As late as the 1980s, the brewery closed down during hunting season so that the staff could go hunting.

Not all of the acquisitions of well regarded independents by mega-brewers resulted in the original brand disappearing or losing its personality. In 1987, Miller Brewing acquired the Jacob Leinenkugel Brewing Company of Chippewa Falls, Wisconsin. Dating back to 1867, the company was a strong regional brand. It was never incorporated into Miller as a subsidiary, but was held autonomously as a separate operating unit, continuing to brew at its own brewery. Ironically, as Miller's sales declined 4.4 percent in the 1990s, those of Leinenkugel — reported separately from Miller — *increased* by 4.3 percent. Listed separately from Miller, Leinenkugel was the eleventh largest brewing company in the United States at the turn of the century.

The tide of consolidation ebbed somewhat in the 1980s for the simple reason that there were fewer breweries left to consolidate. With this turn, the larger breweries that survived turned to an earnest competition for market share. Industry consultants convinced the major brewing companies that the key to more market share was to have more shelf space, and that the key to more shelf space was more products.

Rather than creating new products that were beers in styles other than pale "flavor neutral" lager, the large brewing companies were convinced by their consultants to remain within the lager style and create additional flavor neutral lagers that, if anything, were lighter than the original flagship beer. In retrospect, it seems counter-intuitive that brewers would expand their repertoire by offering consumers less flavor, but apparently having less flavor was a price that a large segment of the market was willing to pay for fewer calories in their beer. Strangely, this counter-intuitive approach to product line extension worked in the mass market in the 1970s and 1980s.

First came "light" beer, a phenomenon that is still with us in the twenty-first century. Reduced-calorie light beer originated as an effort to attract more women as consumers. This genre had been tried a few times in earlier decades, but it returned permanently with "Lite," or Miller Lite, which was first introduced by the Miller Brewing Company in 1975. Anheuser-Busch responded with Budweiser Light (now Bud Light), and soon all major brewing companies added a "light" variant to their product line. There was virtually no major flagship brand anywhere in the United States or Canada that did not also market a companion "light" variant. Stroh introduced a Stroh Light, Coors a Coors Light, Olympia an Olympia Light, and so on. Miller Lite would remain as the largest selling reduced calorie beer in the United States until 1994, when it was eclipsed by Bud Light for the first time.

In the late 1970s, the light beer phenomenon helped to fuel a 7.5 percent increase in overall beer consumption, the largest increase in the United States since World War II. By the mid-1980s, light beers had secured a permanent niche in the North American market, and they accounted for 22 percent of all beer being sold. A light beer typically has between 70 and 100 calories per 12-ounce serving, compared to 150 or more for standard, mass market lagers. This is achieved by

Above: After buying Schlitz, Stroh closed its own brewery in Detroit. (*Collection of the author*)

Above: After many years as a Rocky Mountain regional brand, Colorado's Coors went national. By 1970, it was in the top four in the United States. *(Courtesy of the brewery)*

using less malt and allowing the sugars to ferment more completely. The resulting beer is low on malt and hop flavor, but if served cold, it is perceived as being "clean" and "refreshing," albeit flavor neutral. Miller also noted in its advertising that its Lite — like other lights — was "less filling."

The immense success and market acceptance of reduced-calorie beers prompted some interest among major brewers in marketing reduced-alcohol beers, but the phenomenal success of light beers eight years earlier was not repeated. In the summer of 1989 Anheuser-Busch launched a third wave of new products designed to reach a wider slice of the market with the introduction of their Michelob Dry. By definition, "dry beer" is beer in which all of the fermentable sugars from the original malt have been converted to alcohol. In order to conclude the process with a beer of acceptable alcohol content (roughly 3.2 percent by weight), a brewer must start with less malt. Hence, dry beer had a low original gravity and will have very little flavor unless it is more heavily hopped than typical beers. The process is similar to that used by brewers to produce light beer, and the results are very similar. In

fact, most American mass market lagers, including light and dry beers, were very similar in taste.

In the early 1990s, the short-lived "dry" beer craze was superseded by the "ice" beer marketing phenomenon. Like "dry" beer, "ice" beer was merely a subtle variation of very lightly-flavored lager. Developed and patented by Labatt in Canada, it is a process by which beer is quickly chilled to sub-freezing temperatures after brewing but before final fermentation. The result is the formation of ice crystals in the beer, which are removed to produce a beer with roughly *twice* the alcohol content of typical mass market lagers. As they had with "light" and "dry" beers, most major companies introduced an "ice" version of their major products. Though heavily marketed, neither the "dry" nor "ice" product variants survived long, nor achieved the market success that "light" beers had.

Even as the major national brewing giants, as well as many large regionals, were embracing the flavor neutral dogma during the 1980s, a new strata of breweries was emerging at the grassroots level with exactly the opposite approach. Instead of giving consumers less, they offered the consumer *more*.

Left: A sampling of products and product variants from Anheuser-Busch and Miller Brewing, America's top two brewing companies since the 1980s.
Below: A young lady enjoys a Pilsner glass of classic American lager. (*Collection of the author*)

Chapter 6

AMERICAN BREWERY RENAISSANCE

AMERICA'S BABY BOOM GENERATION grew up in a prosperous and expanding society, coming of age as many consumer product industries, including the brewing industry, experienced both growth and round after round of mergers and consolidations. As hometown and small regional breweries faded away, the notion of local pride in the local beer became a remote relic of their grandparents' era. Tastes had changed.

Today, we remember the 1950s and early 1960s as an era of blandness, and this was certainly the case with beer. For the national brewers, the idea of flavor neutral beer went hand in hand with multi-site brewing. The more flavor neu-

tral the product, the more fail safe it is to achieve a uniform and consistent flavor while brewing simultaneously in diverse corners of the country, such as in New York, Missouri and California.

In the case of brewing, there was a reason for the blandness. In order to maintain consistency at many locations, it was desirable to reduce the complexity and character of the ingredients that affect product's flavor, in other words, to make the product flavor neutral. Schlitz, for example, apologetically advertised its beer as having "just a kiss of hops," as though hop flavor had become a bad thing.

To compete with the burgeoning national brands, many regional brewers found themselves matching the flavor neutral example of the national brands. With the flavor of the beer becoming less complex and more homogeneous, the consumer criteria became price rather than flavor. This put them into a corner, because it is axiomatically difficult for a small-scale business to compete with a large-scale business on the basis of price. As we have seen, one by one, they failed or found themselves consolidated into a larger entity. During the 1970s, the number of breweries it the United States had dwindled to fewer than 50 and the biggest three national brands came to own most of the brewing facilities, and virtually all of the brewing capacity.

The breweries were fewer and fewer, but it mattered little because the beer varied so little. The baby boomers grew up watching their parents vote for Miss Rheingold, or watching the antics of the Hamm's bear on television — the 1950s and 1960s may have been an era of blandness in beer, but they were a golden age for advertising. The icons of advertising gave products their identity, but unfortunately, the brewery icons were more distinctive that the beers that they represented.

America's baby boom generation, who reached adulthood in a comfortable and

Opposite: **The brewhouse at Sierra Nevada.** (*Courtesy of the brewery*) **Above:** Fritz Maytag. (*Terry McCarthy photo via Anchor Brewing*)

Left: The Anchor Steam Beer label.
Below: Fritz Maytag at work in the Anchor Brewery on Eighth Street in San Francisco. The brewery subsequently moved to larger quarters on nearby Mariposa Street. (*Courtesy of Anchor Brewing*)

gradually more homogeneous society, was growing anxious for the exceptional. In the 1960s, they found it in their fashion, their music and their culture. Eventually, this same generation would also seek and find the exceptional in their beer.

Gradually tastes were changing — again. Why not, it was asked, compete with the national brands on quality and flavor, rather than on quantity and price?

It was in 1965, that a recent Stanford University graduate named Fritz Maytag was given some startling news. The San Francisco brewery that brewed his favorite beer was about to go out of business. Dating back to 1896, the Anchor Brewing Company was typical of the hundreds of local breweries that had survived Prohibition only to be buried by the tide of mass merchandising that had created the national brands. For the price of a used car, Maytag bought a controlling interest in Anchor in 1965. The combination of chemistry, business and tradition had an intoxicating effect on him. "I was made for this brewery," he once told an interviewer. "It was a marriage made in heaven."

Though it would be a decade before the business was profitable, Fritz Maytag had seen to it that Anchor did not simply fade away. He also bought himself a career

that would define the rest of his life, as well as the future of small-scale brewing in the United States.

Writing in the early 1960s, Stanley Baron observed that "The phenomenon of brewery mortality (called euphemistically a 'shakedown' by industrial analysts) has been constantly evident ever since Repeal. . . . The trend toward larger and larger groupings of brewing companies is an undeniable fact, though it might best be seen as a tendency within industry in general. During the 1950s, such combines have emerged in the railroad industry, in banking, in airlines, in the hotel business, in publishing — to mention only a few. While this is still going on, one cannot draw any firm conclusions about its significance for the future. Contemporary problems of financing, of public relations and promotion, in addition to an increasing uniformity of taste and activity which is brought about by better and closer communications, may be doing away with all that is local and independent. The sociologists will have to decide in the end whether this is a good or bad thing."

The issue of "increasing uniformity of taste" that Baron left to the sociologists to decide in 1962, would be taken up nearly two decades later, not by sociologists, but by beer drinkers and a new generation of brewers. Citing Fritz Maytag as their inspiration, a new breed of "craft brewers" came on the scene with the novel notion that beer should be carefully crafted rather than mass produced. Ingredients should be selected to enhance flavor rather than disguise flavor. At a time when many brewing companies were cutting corners by such tactics as substituting corn and rice for barley, Maytag threw himself into maintaining and nurturing the highest quality beer possible.

The craft brewers adopted his approach as their credo. "In the beer world, the word revered would not be overdone," Lew Bryson, managing editor of *Malt Advocate* magazine said of Maytag. "Everybody outside the [mega-brewers] owes him a debt."

Just as the "increasing uniformity of taste" trend was reversed, so too was the downward spiral in the numbers of breweries. Beginning on the West Coast, new brewing companies were starting to appear. They were important to the history of American brewing because they represented a fresh approach to regional beer and brewing. It was fresh, but not new. It was reminiscent of a way Americans had looked at beer and brewing in the nine-

teenth century and in the twentieth century before Prohibition. The new generation of brewers looked upon brewing as an art rather than as a factory chore. They thought of themselves as chefs, rather than as factory managers. The new breweries were small, but they were commercially viable, and they had a strong local acceptance. Because they were typically much smaller than a traditional brewery, the name "microbrewery" was adopted.

The craft brewing movement would give Americans a vastly wider selection of styles and varieties of fresh, domestically produced beers than had been available since the nineteenth century. Craft brewing also signaled a return to the concept of regional, and even neighborhood, breweries, an idea that was thought to have perished soon after the end of World War II.

With the advent of the microbreweries, a new generation began to discover and take pride in local brews, just as their grandparents had. For the first time in over a century, the number of brewing companies in North America began to increase. In the United States the number of breweries went from fewer than 50 in 1980 to 190 in 1988.

The first of the new microbreweries was New Albion Brewing, founded in

Above: Boulder Brewing Company was Colorado's first microbrewery. It was founded in a goat shed in 1979 by two homebrewing university professors who were granted the 43rd brewing license in the United States at the time. Incorporated in May 1980, it began brewing in this, its current facility, five years later. Between 1993 and 2004, the company was known Rockies Brewing, but readopted the earlier name to get back to its roots. (*Courtesy of the brewery*)

Above: A selection of classic product labels from Sierra Nevada Brewing. Pale Ale is the flagship brand, Celebration the winter seasonal brand. (*Courtesy of the brewery*)

1976 by Jack McAuliffe in Sonoma, California, about 90 minutes north of San Francisco where Fritz Maytag was working to transform Anchor. Though New Albion would not survive the decade, McAuliffe's experiment served as the prototype for a new generation of microbreweries. After New Albion, it would be several years before the craft brewing movement began to spread. By 1980, River City Brewing opened in Sacramento, California and Sierra Nevada Brewing opened in nearby Chico. Founded by homebrewers Ken Grossman and Paul Camusi, Sierra Nevada was established in 1979, with the first beer being sold in February 1981. While River City survived only a few years, Sierra Nevada is now

one of the largest brewing companies in North America.

The craft beer revolution spread to Colorado in 1980 with the opening of the Boulder Brewing Company (Rockies Brewing from 1993 to 2004), and to New York state as William Newman began brewing in Albany the following year. Two important microbreweries opened in Washington state during 1982. These were Paul Shipman's Redhook Ale Brewery in Seattle and Bert Grant's Yakima Brewing & Malting, which was located in Yakima, Washington, the heart of one of the most important hop-growing regions in North America.

Meanwhile, during his first two decades, Fritz Maytag increased Anchor Brewing's output 75-fold. The company's flagship product is Anchor Steam Beer, which has become one of America's most prized premium beers. It was developed by master brewer Maytag himself, and is loosely based on what little is known of the legendary "steam" beers produced in gold rush days. "Steam" has long been a trademark of Anchor Brewing. Other Anchor products include Anchor Porter, Anchor Liberty Ale, and Old Foghorn Barley Wine-style Ale, which was first produced in 1975. Anchor is renowned locally for its annual Christmas beer, which has been specially brewed since 1975, with a different recipe each year.

The original definition of a microbrewery was a brewery with a capacity of less than 3,000 barrels, but by the end of the 1980s this threshold increased to 15,000 barrels as the demand for microbrewed beer first doubled, and then tripled. Meanwhile, another new entity born of the craft brewing revolution was the "brewpub," a microbrewery that both brewed *and* served its beer to the public on the same premises. Unlike a microbrewery the primary market for the products of a brewpub is under its own roof. By definition, a brewpub brews to serve. Some brewpubs would bottle their beers for sale to patrons and for wholesale to retailers, while some microbreweries would also operate brewpubs, so the distinction between the two is somewhat blurred. Both, however, share a commitment to their own unique beers, and most brewpublicans entered their trade out of a love for brewing and an interest in distinctive beer styles.

Brewpubs had existed in the United States in the eighteenth and nineteenth centuries. However, after Prohibition, it was illegal in most states and Canadian provinces to both brew beer and sell it

directly to the public on the same site. Changes in local laws since the early 1980s rescinded these outdated restrictions and have made it possible for brewpubs to become widespread.

In Yakima, Bert Grant would open America's first brewpub in more than a century in 1982, and others soon followed. Mendocino Brewing, which was established in the appropriately-named village of Hopland, about two hours north of San Francisco, opened in 1983, and was followed by Buffalo Bill Owens' brewpub in Hayward, across the Bay from San Francisco. By the time that Allen Paul opened San Francisco Brewing in the old Albatross Saloon in 1986, there was a rush of new brewpubs opening throughout the United States. Mike and Brian McMenamin led the brewpub revolution into the Northwest in 1985 with the Hillsdale in Portland, and within four years they had opened six brewpubs in western Oregon.

In the last quarter of the twentieth century, the first generation of American brewpubs set a benchmark for general ambiance that is still common in the twenty-first century. Brewpubs were generally small, comfortable, informal venues, with the look and feel of traditional neighborhood bars. They were usually decorated

Above: To achieve the complex hop character that is Sierra Nevada's trademark, brewers add different varieties of whole hops to the brew kettles at specific points during the boil. Their Bigfoot Ale, Celebration Ale, and other specialty beers receive an additional dry-hopping during the maturation period. (*Courtesy of the brewery*)

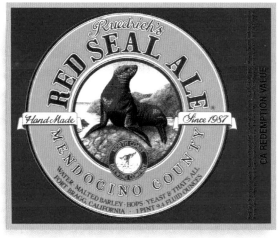

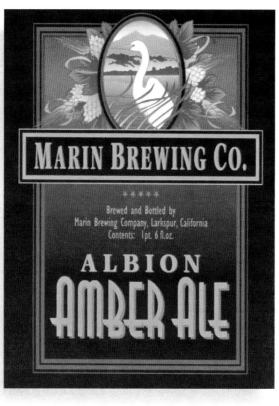

Above: **Products from classic California craft brewers, including (***clockwise from left***) North Coast in Fort Bragg, Stanislaus in Modesto, Marin in Larkspur and Mendocino, born in Hopland and now in Ukiah. (***Courtesy of the breweries***)**

with local historical ephemera or beer and brewing memorabilia. If food was served, it usually consisted of sandwiches, burgers and snacks. The overall emphasis of the brewpubs was on the reason that they were created in the first place — beer. Everything else about the theme and the feel of the place was designed to support and enhance that central feature.

One aspect of the craft brewing revolution that cannot be overemphasized is that of the introduction — or re-introduction — of a variety of specialty beer styles. With the craft brewing movement, beer lovers suddenly had unfettered access to

rich amber ale, opaque stouts and true Pilsen-style lagers. These were made the way that they actually made them in Pilsen. Making beers that were "flavor neutral" was the last thing the craft brewers wanted to accomplish.

Beer styles that most Americans had never heard of were suddenly available. In Modesto, California, Stanislaus Brewing introduced St. Stan's Altbier, a style of beer that then existed in and around Dusseldorf, Germany, but nowhere else. Fruit beers, found in Belgium and virtually nowhere else until after 1980, cropped up at craft brewing operations in the United States from Oregon to Wisconsin by the mid-1980s. In Portland, Oregon, Kurt and Rob Widmer, who founded Widmer Brothers Brewing Company in 1984, went on to pioneer an American variation on the German hefeweizen (wheat beer) in 1986. They were also among the first breweries to introduce seasonal beers — other than Christmas beers — into America.

The new microbreweries were not the only institutions that would benefit from Fritz Maytag's bold experiment. Among the other beneficiaries of the interest in craft brewed beer were the other independent regional brewers who, like Anchor, had been bucking the consolidation trend for decades. Just as beer drinkers were discovering a new generation of brewers who were recapturing a beer and brewing styles that were an homage to the brewers of their grandfathers' day, others were enjoying beer from the same breweries that had supplied their grandparents. A case in point is D.G. Yuengling Brewing Company of Pottsville, Pennsylvania. Having been founded in 1829, the oldest brewery in the United States could well have brewed the beer enjoyed by our great great grandparents. In 1985, as the craft brewing movement was just beginning to sweep the country, Richard L. "Dick" Yuengling bought the family "microbrewery" from his father. He had big plans. In 1992, the brewery began the largest expansion in its 165-year history, and by 1997, the Pottsville brewery was producing over 500,000 barrels annually and exceeding its capacity.

The brewery's success was a corollary to the success of the craft brewing movement. Dick Yuengling was able to capitalize on many of the same features that consumers found attractive with microbrews — a quality product from a small, family-run brewery, and a strong local following. It was pointed out in *Modern Brewery Age*

magazine that "Pennsylvanians are the most loyal beer consumers in the country, and they have embraced Yuengling as their own." While the statement may not be true of Pennsylvania — Oregonians would certainly take exception — it was true of Yuengling. As the industry publication pointed out, Yuengling Brewing has "worked on building extraordinary depth in its home state."

Also on the short list — the very short list — of family-owned regional breweries was August Schell Brewing in New Ulm, Minnesota. August Schell has a history similar to that of Yuengling, although it is a considerably newer company. Schell was not started until 1860, the year that Abraham Lincoln was campaigning for his first term in the White House. When Schell opened its doors, Yuengling had been brewing for more than a quarter of a century. Nevertheless, both companies survived the Civil War, Prohibition and the Consolidation era as independents with a strong local following. In 1988 the Great American Beer Festival called August Schell Pilsner "unquestionably America's finest Pilsner beer."

Like Yuengling, Schell and Anchor, another small, still independent nineteenth century brewery that has flourished

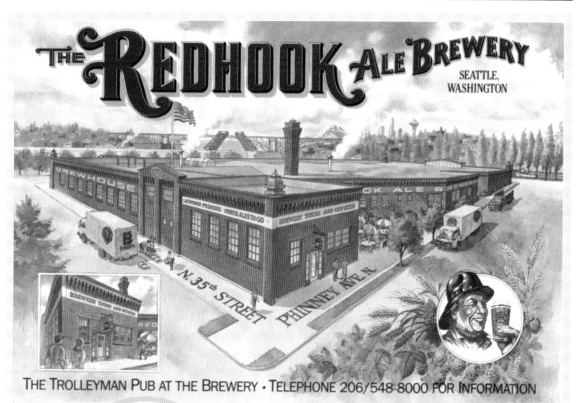

THE TROLLEYMAN PUB AT THE BREWERY · TELEPHONE 206/548-8000 FOR INFORMATION

Above: **An early Redhook advertising card.** *Left:* **The classic label for Redhook's flagship beer.** (*Courtesy of the brewery*)

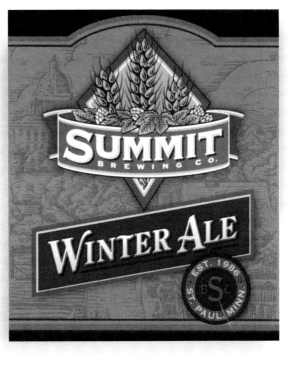

Above and left: **Products from great craft and regional brewers in the upper Midwest, including Stevens Point in Stevens Point, Lakefront in Milwaukee and Summit in St. Paul.** (*Courtesy of the breweries*)

in the craft beer environment of the twenty-first century is the Stevens Point Brewery in the Wisconsin city of the same name. Indeed, at the 2003 Great American Beer Festival, Point Special Lager won the Gold Medal in the American Premium Lager category, triumphing over Miller Genuine Draft and Budweiser. Point beer was sold exclusively in Wisconsin for the brewery's first 133 years of operation, but the company began selling its brands in neighboring Minnesota in 1990, and in Illinois the following year. Indiana and

Michigan were added in 2004. In the meantime, Stevens Point acquired the Augsberger brand from Stroh in 2003, and the classic Augsburger Beers were reintroduced in Wisconsin and Illinois. In 2005, Stevens Point purchased the James Page Brewing Company, a Minneapolis craft brewery founded by James Page in 1986. The James Page brands included Iron Range Amber, Burly Brown, Voyageur Extra Pale Ale, and White Ox Wheat Ale. To its own year-round product line, Stevens Point added Point Honey Light and White Bière in 2002, and in 2005, the brewery introduced three gourmet soda brands. In 2007, Stevens Point celebrated its 150th anniversary.

Another nineteenth century brewer who enjoyed a bit of brand rejuvenation in the 1980s and early 1990s was Latrobe Brewing, located in the Pennsylvania town of the same name. It was established in 1893 at a time when the town's only other brewery was located at St. Vincent's Abbey and operated by Benedictine monks. The brewery at St Vincent's closed in 1898 after 42 years of operation, but the brewery that took the name of the town survived. The flagship Rolling Rock brand is named for the nearby Rolling Rock Estate, a horse ranch. An intriguing detail about Rolling Rock is the presence of the mysterious "33" symbol that appears on the back of the bottle. In was noted during that 1980s, that no one at the company itself could remember why it was put there in the first place — because the product was introduced in 1939. Numerous contests have been held through the years to come up with clever solutions to the conundrum. In 1987, Latrobe Brewing was acquired by Labatt Breweries, then Canada's largest brewing company. In 1995, Labatt was, in turn, acquired by Interbrew (now known as InBev), a Belgium-based company that later became the world's largest brewery holding company, with operations spanning Europe and the Asia-Pacific region.

While many early microbrewers came to the business with an interest in the art of brewing, other entrepreneurs joined this new generation out of an interest in merchandising and branding. The entrepreneurs formed virtual brewing companies, or brewing companies without a brewery. They marketed a brand, but contracted with another brewing company to actually produce the beer. This process was called "contract brewing." The use of contract brewing allowed many entrepreneurs with ideas for products to get them on the shelf without having to construct breweries.

Contract brewing first emerged in the 1980s in the major markets of the Northeast. Philadelphia, New York and Boston each saw the development of a major local brand that was actually brewed under contract somewhere else.

One of the first and best known entrepreneurs to use contract brewing was Jim Koch of Boston, who formed his Boston Beer Company in 1985 to produce Samuel Adams Lager. His idea was to create an American beer — named for the eighteenth century Boston patriot and maltster — which could compete with the best German beers and pass the Reinheitsgebot (German Purity Law). "Sam Adams" passed the test and was actually sold in West Germany before Koch had expanded his marketing in the United States beyond the Boston area. Having contract brewed his beer in Pennsylvania initially, Koch acquired and renovated the former Haffenreffer Brewery in an old brewing neighborhood in Boston, and began brewing part of the Boston Beer output at that site in 1988. By the early 1990s, Sam Adams was available throughout the United States.

Below: Two classic products from Stevens Point. *Left:* Two of Iowa's craft breweries, Dallas County Brewing (Old Depot) in Adel and Cedar Brewing in Cedar Rapids. (*Courtesy of the breweries*)

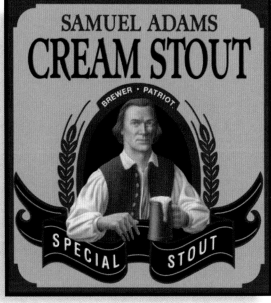

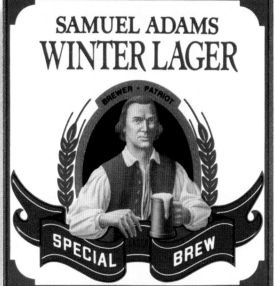

Above and right: **Classic early labels from the product portfolio of Jim Koch's Boston Beer Company.** (*Courtesy of the breweries*)

New York City's first new brewing companies after the craft brewing movement began were Old New York, whose Amsterdam Amber was brewed under contract by F.X. Matt Brewing in Utica, in upstate New York, and Manhattan Brewing, a brewpub. Robert D'Addona started the now defunct Manhattan Brewing in 1984 in a former Consolidated Edison substation on Thompson Street in the city's Soho district.

In Utica, F.X. Matt, also known as West End Brewing, would evolve into one of the largest of the contract brewers in the East during the late 1980s and early 1990s. Originally founded in 1853, the company that had long been famous for its own Utica Club brand would contract brew for a number of eastern companies during the 1980s and 1990s. During the 1950s and 1960s, the brewery produced as much as 600,000 barrels annually of the Utica Club and Matt's Premium flagship beers, but, like many smaller brewing companies, it had suffered a gradual decline of these traditional brands in the 1970s and 1980s. For Matt, the specialty beer wave arrived in the nick of time. Francis Xavier Matt II, who took the helm of the family business in 1980, re-invented the company, replacing declining brands with con-

Philadelphia's initial microbrewery "house" brands — Jeff Ware's Dock Street and Tom Pastorius's Pennsylvania Pilsner — were originally contract brewed, but Pastorius opened his own brewery in Pittsburgh in 1989. Two other early contract brewing companies in leading eastern markets were the Brooklyn Brewery, which was founded in 1988, and Olde Heurich Brewing in Washington, DC, which was founded by Gary Heurich, grandson of Christian Heurich, who had built his brewery in 1873 on the site where the Kennedy Center now stands.

tract brewing and with the best-selling Saranac specialty line.

Of course, contract brewing was not confined to the Northeast. Montana Beverages of Helena, a microbrewery founded in 1982, brewed not only its own Kessler brand, but also produced products for brewing companies throughout the West.

Meanwhile, just as contract brewing was not confined to the East, neither were all of the new brewers in the East contract brewers. William Newman had led the way in Albany, and Robert D'Addona followed in Manhattan. Among the first outside the Empire State were D.L. Geary Brewing in Portland, Maine and Catamount Brewing in White River Junction, Vermont, which opened in 1986 and 1987 respectively. Another early Eastern micro was Mass Bay Brewing — famous for the Harpoon brand — which began brewing in Boston in 1987, and which was among the top ten specialty brewers in the United States at the turn of the century.

The proliferation of new breweries changed the face of American brewing. In an interview in *Modern Brewery Age*, William Coors recalled that in 1965, he told Henry King, head of the United States Brewers' Association, that "if the industry continued the way it was going,

by the millennium we would be down to five breweries. I was simply extrapolating the death curve out. I didn't take into account this eruption of pub and boutique breweries. I think it's the best thing that has happened to the brewing industry, if you really want to know. . . it definitely adds to the cultural acceptance of beer."

Right and below: **Classic products from among the first generation of craft brewers in the Northeast, including Catamount in Vermont, Manhattan in New York City, Penn Pilsner in Pittsburgh and Dock Street in Philadelphia.** (*Courtesy of the breweries*)

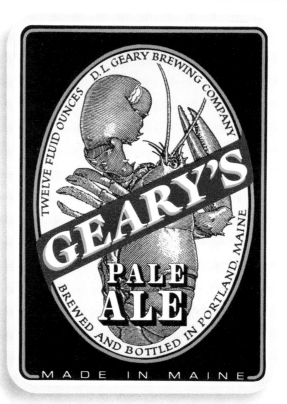

Above and right: Classic products from New England craft brewers include Harpoon in Boston; Geary's in Maine; and Otter Creek in Middlebury, Vermont. The latter also produces Wolaver's Certified Organic Ales.

Opposite: A selection of raspberry beers from Mad Anthony in Indiana, Lost Coast in California and the late Oldenberg Brewery in Kentucky. (*Courtesy of the breweries*)

Main picture opposite: Oldenberg's vintage delivery truck. (*Bill Yenne photo*)

Between 1980 and 1995, the number of breweries in the United States grew more than tenfold, from fewer than 50 to 500, the highest number since World War II. The following year, it was noted that there were more breweries in the United States than in Germany. According to the Institute of Brewing Studies, the number nearly tripled to more that 1,400 in the first years of the twenty-first century. This brought the total number of breweries back to a level that had not been seen since the first years of the previous century.

Even as the craft brewers were flourishing, their market share reflected the choice of the prefix "micro" in microbrewery. At the upper end of the scale, the big four American brewers controlled 83 percent of the total domestic market. Number one Anheuser-Busch controlled more that 50 percent of the total domestic market at the turn of the century, up from 42 percent in 1990 and 28 percent in 1980. Certainly, Anheuser-Busch grew so robustly to become such a monumental industry presence that it is clearly the twentieth century's success story in United States brewing. Still reflecting the expansive 1876 vision of Adolphus Busch, the company had evolved into a well-integrated corporation with a diversification that ranges from theme parks to major-league sports. At the beginning of the twentieth century, the industry buzzed about million-barrel brewers. A century later, Anheuser-Busch was the world's first *hundred million* barrel brewer with sales of 98 million barrels in the United States in 2000, and 105 million barrels worldwide.

Rounding out the big five in the early 1990s were Miller Brewing in second place, followed by Stroh Brewing (which had incorporated Schlitz in 1982), Coors and Heileman.

While Anheuser-Busch would remain aloof and above the fray during the 1990s, big changes would be in store for the other four. Miller would spend the decade rediscovering itself and introducing new brands. Plank Road, the original name of the brewery that Fred Miller bought from the Best Brothers in 1853, had been revived briefly in the mid-1980s as a Miller brand. A decade later, in 1994, the name resurfaced as Miller's "Plank Road Brewery" began brewing the Red Dog and Icehouse brands. In 1997-1998 Miller revived its decades-old "Miller Time" advertising slogan and brought back the long-abandoned "Girl-in-the-Moon" logo that had originated in the nineteenth century. On the business and marketing side, Miller had bought, then sold, a 20 percent stake in Molson Breweries of Canada

between 1993 and 1997. A decade later Molson would merge with Coors.

After their much heralded rise to prominence through acquisitions, Stroh and Heileman had both moved into the top five and were enjoying solid growth in the 1980s. Between them, the two brewers controlled 40 percent of the United States market as the 1990s began. Soon, it would be a different story. Alan Bond had financed his 1987 acquisition of Heileman with junk bonds and his empire

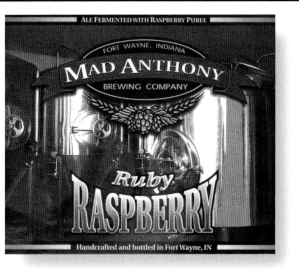

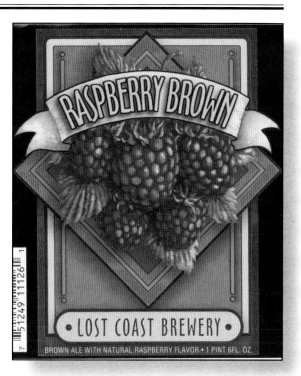

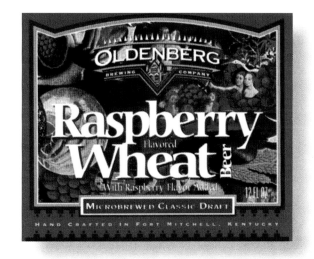

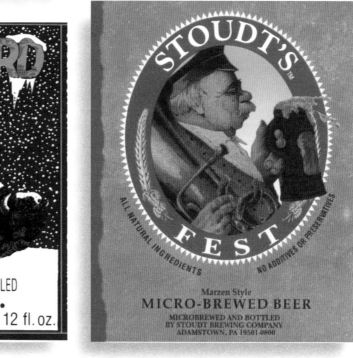

Clockwise from above: Classic craft beers from around the United States include Wasatch from Schirf Brewing in Utah, Buffalo Gold from Rockies (now Boulder) Brewing in Colorado, Abita Bock from Abita Brewing in Louisiana, Fest from Stoudt Brewing in Pennsylvania, and Blizzard Bock from Buffalo Brewing in upstate New York. *Opposite:* The flagship Double Barrel brand from Firestone Walker in Paso Robles, California. *(Courtesy of the breweries)*

collapsed in 1991, and this sent Heileman into bankruptcy.

In the summer of 1996, Stroh acquired Heileman's five breweries, including the main Heileman plant in LaCrosse, Wisconsin, as well as Blitz-Weinhard in Portland and Rainier in Seattle, along with the Heileman-owned brands, such as Special Export, Old Style, Rainier, Henry Weinhard and Lone Star. In the meantime, Heileman had sold its Grain Belt brand and the Schmidt brewery in St. Paul to the Minnesota Brewing Company.

Within a few years of swallowing Heileman, however, the cachet of Stroh's large portfolio of brands had faded somewhat. A major part of the company's business was now contract brewing for the likes of Boston Beer Company, purveyors of the fast-growing Samuel Adams brand — as well as for Pabst.

In 1999, when Jim Koch of Boston Beer decided to pull out of Stroh and move to Miller Brewing, John Stroh III announced that the Stroh family would be pulling the plug on the family business a year short of its 150th birthday.

This set the stage for what some brewing industry analysts referred to as "the final consolidation" of 1999. This phrase was obviously eve-of-the-millennium hyperbole, but clearly the implosion of Stroh (with the Heileman brands included), sent dominoes tumbling. In turn, this affected both Miller and Pabst in what was the biggest series of changes to hit the top end of the industry since the 1970s.

Pabst, the biggest name in American brewing at the beginning of the twentieth century had faded after its acquisition by Paul Kalmanovitz in 1985, along with the Falstaff, Olympia and Hamm's brand names which it owned. When Kalmanovitz died in 1987, the obituary for Pabst had already been written and was ready to run. However, Lutz Issleib, the new Pabst president, undertook to turn the company around.

In 1999, when the Stroh family decided to get out of the brewing business altogether, Pabst bought most of Stroh's brands and breweries, although Miller acquired the Henry Weinhard and Blitz-Weinhard brands, along with the magnificent old Weinhard brewery building in downtown Portland. Miller kept the brands, but the building was recycled as an office building.

Pabst, in turn, sold the Hamm's brand and the big former Olympia brewery at Tumwater — but not the Olympia brand — to Miller. The final consolidation left the Tumwater facility as the largest brewery by far in the Northwest. Its two biggest rivals — the Rainier Brewery in Seattle and the Blitz-Weinhard Brewery in Portland — were both Heileman properties that were passed to Stroh and closed in 1999.

Having shed itself of Hamm's and letting Miller take the Weinhard name, Pabst now owned the rest of the surviving former Heileman and Stroh brand names. The "Heileman" name was retained in the case of the company's former flagship brands, which were still called "Heileman's" Old Style and "Heileman's" Special Export. Other familiar regional brands that Heileman or Paul Kalmanovitz had "collected" over the years remained officially alive, although they were no longer brewed in the regions that made them significant. These included such household names as Blatz, Falstaff, Heidelberg, Lucky Lager, Piel, Rainier, Schmidt's, Stag and the former New York area giants, Ballantine and Schaefer. Most of the brewing plants — from the Rainier facility in Seattle to the Stroh brewery in Winston-Salem — were closed or sold by August 1999.

Pabst contracted with Miller to brew Olympia, and ironically, the Oly brand continued to be brewed at the original

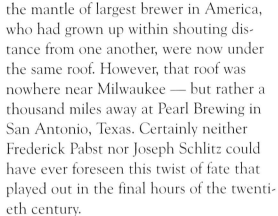

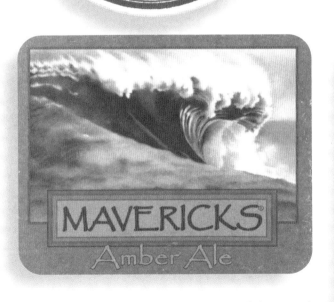

Favorite brewpubs, clockwise from top left: Heartland in New York City; Great Northern in Whitefish, Montana; Twenty Tank in San Francisco; San Francisco Brewing; and Half Moon Bay in Princeton, California. (*Collection of the author*)

source in Tumwater even though the brand and brewery were owned separately.

Pabst also now owned Lone Star, the erstwhile "National Beer of Texas," which was bought by Olympia of Washington in 1976 and by Heileman of Wisconsin in 1983. Pabst would brew the beer in the Lone Star State — not at the massive Lone Star brewery on the south side of San Antonio, but at the Pearl Brewing facility on the north side of town, which had been owned by Pabst since 1988. Both Pearl and Lone Star, the former cross-town rivals, were produced at the same facility.

By acquiring the Stroh portfolio, Pabst also now owned the Schlitz brand. Ironically, the two former Milwaukee rivals for the mantle of largest brewer in America, who had grown up within shouting distance from one another, were now under the same roof. However, that roof was nowhere near Milwaukee — but rather a thousand miles away at Pearl Brewing in San Antonio, Texas. Certainly neither Frederick Pabst nor Joseph Schlitz could have ever foreseen this twist of fate that played out in the final hours of the twentieth century.

As it turned out, the "final consolidation" of 1999 was not final at all. Of the big three brewers at the beginning of the twenty-first century, two — Miller and Coors — would change hands within five years, and the fourth place brewer — Pabst — would stop brewing its own beer entirely. In 2002, after 33 years in the portfolio of tobacco giant Philip Morris, Miller was sold to a brewing company. On May 30, 2002, it was announced that London-based South African Breweries (SAB) had agreed to buy Miller from Philip Morris for $5.6 billion. The acquisition created what was then the world's second-largest brewing company behind Anheuser-Busch, knocking Heineken out of second place for the first time in decades. The name of this new entity would be "SABMiller."

South African Breweries had become the world's fourth largest brewing company in the same manner that Heileman had become the fifth largest American brewer in the 1980s — through acquisition. SAB, known in Africa for its well-established Castle brand, is a consortium formed in 1895. It had worked its way into a place as the largest brewing company in Africa during the mid-twentieth century and had entered the world market through the acquisitions of companies such as Pilsner Urquell in the Czech Republic. By the 1990s, SAB was also the largest non-Chinese brewer in China. With Miller in the portfolio, the merged company moved ahead of Heineken as the world's third largest brewing company (after InBev and Anheuser-Busch).

At Tumwater in Washington, Miller had declared in October 1999 that it intended to construct facilities that would more than double the plant's million-barrel annual output. However, the seeds of its demise had already been sewn in an intrigue involving the very thing upon which the brewery had been founded, the water. In January 2000, Miller announced that it wanted to manage wastewater from the brewery and sell unused capacity back to the local water department that had the

water treatment contract. Many months of discussion followed before the two parties finally reached an agreement. However, in November 2001, the Washington Department of Ecology denied Miller a permit to discharge its own treated wastewater. In January 2003, Miller, now part of SAB-Miller, announced that the Tumwater brewery would not be expanded, but rather it would be closed. The reason was that the company could not "justify the cost of its operations." The Tumwater brewery was officially closed in June 2003. The artesian water that Leopold Schmidt had discovered a century before still flowed, but it flowed untapped for brewing beer.

When the Tumwater brewery closed, it left a microbrewery, the Redhook Ale Brewery of suburban Seattle, as the largest brewery in the Northwest. Redhook had brewed 225,000 barrels in 2002, compared to 1.7 million at Tumwater.

Meanwhile, SABMiller turned to a former microbrewery to brew the Henry Weinhard brands that it had acquired as part of the 1999 "final consolidation." Henry Weinhard beer had been established as strong regional premium brand in the West through intensive advertising

Left: **The distinctive label from Mike Levis's Santa Fe Brewing in Galisteo, New Mexico.** (*Courtesy of the brewery*)

Above: **The classic form of point-of-sale beer advertising, coasters are used to promote brands, brewpubs such as Triple Rock, and even beer festivals.** (*Collection of the author*)

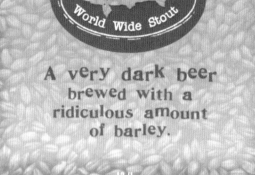

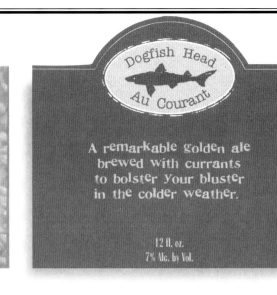

Above: The Dogfish Head Brewery was started in Milton, Delaware in 1995. It specializes in what are described as experimental or extreme beers that are widely popular in the Chesapeake Bay Area.
Right: The original, short-lived Coeur d'Alene Brewing started in the Idaho city of the same name in 1908, and the current incarnation was born in 1987 as T.W. Fisher's, a Brewpub. Huckleberries are the signature berry of the Idaho panhandle and western Montana. (Courtesy of the breweries)

in the 1970s and 1980s, and still had a faithful following, so SABMiller contracted with Full Sail Brewing Company, an employee-owned company in Hood River, Oregon. One of the first of Oregon's microbreweries, Full Sail was already distributing its own beers in fifteen states by the turn of the century. Beginning in July 2003, Full Sail began brewing three beers for SABMiller under the Henry Weinhard brand. Though it did not have stock in Full Sail, SABMiller did make capital investments in

the brewery as part of the agreement to brew Henry Weinhard beers.

In February 2005, in another postscript to 1999's not-so-final consolidation, Coors joined forces with Molson — Canada's largest brewer — to form the Molson Coors Brewing Company, which was then the world's fifth largest brewer by volume with 41.2 million barrels sold in 2005. Coors remained the third largest brewer in the United States and the Coors brewery in Golden, Colorado remained the world's largest single brewing plant.

Meanwhile, in December 2002, however, Pabst, the one-time largest brewer in America ceased to brew beer entirely. From the beginning of 2003, Pabst became a "virtual brewer." The former Pearl Brewery was sold, and all of the Pabst brands sent hither and yon to be contract brewed by other companies elsewhere. In a twist that continued to link Pabst and Miller, the majority of the brands would be brewed by Miller. Pearl and Lone Star, for example, were still produced in Texas — at Miller's facility in Fort Worth.

As the century ended amid the settling dust of the "final consolidation," the statistics revealed a mixed picture of industry growth among mega-brewers during the 1990s. Number one Anheuser-Busch posted a modest 13.6 increase in sales, while Miller actually declined 4.4 percent, and Coors grew 19.8 percent. Pabst, meanwhile, leaped into fourth place from being number six in the 1980s, and its large acquisitions helped it grow by 66.7 percent. In fifth place was Genesee, the old upstate New York regional, who had been in seventh place in the 1980s. Genesee moved up two notches simply because two of the previous decade's big six — Stroh and Heileman — had just gone away. In fact, sales for Genesee declined 38.6 percent in the 1990s.

The craft brewing segment, meanwhile, enjoyed steady annual growth of 40 to 50 percent through most of the 1990s, until the recession of 1997-1998. At that point, an industry shake-out led to a large number of well-publicized closings of marginal microbrewery operations. In Darwinian fashion, the stronger craft brewers weathered the storm and grew stronger, while the weak closed their doors. Those who had characterized the craft brewing movement as a fad in the 1980s were quick to proclaim the end of microbreweries. However, like the much-heralded obituaries of Mark Twain and Rock & Roll, these epitaphs were more than premature.

Gary Fish, who established the Deschutes Brewery & Public House as a small brewpub in Bend, Oregon in 1988 — and later built it into one of the largest breweries in the Northwest — is a case in point of the staying power of craft breweries. Said Fish of the maturing craft brew market of the 1990s, "This industry has more credibility now. . . It has grown, and the quality of the beer has improved. Failures are just business, not a fad gone awry. We think there are very good times to come for this segment of the industry."

During the 1990s, when the overall output of the American brewing industry remained flat, the growth of the craft beer segment was remarkable. D.G. Yuengling posted an increase of 569.6 percent for the decade, and putting it into the top five by 2005 with 1.57 million barrels. To meet the demand, Yuengling acquired the former Stroh brewery in Tampa, Florida in 1999, and constructed a new million-barrel brewery at St. Clair, a few miles northeast of Pottsville, which opened in 2001. During the 1990s, Jim Koch's Boston Beer Company was up 1,008 percent and Sierra Nevada Brewing Company leapt from 30th place to ninth among all American brewing companies with an increase of more than 1,500 percent.

Left: When Rheingold was reintroduced, Kate Duyn reigned in 2003 as the first Miss Rheingold since Sharon Vaughn in 1965. *(Both pictures are courtesy of Terry Liebman, Rheingold Brewing)*

Above: The classic labels for the Amber Ale and Winter "Wassail" from Full Sail Brewing in Hood River, Oregon. *Above right:* The subsequent, redesigned Wassail label. *Opposite:* The Deschutes Brewing Public House in Bend, Oregon and a label for the brewery's popular Black Butte Porter. (*Courtesy of the breweries*)

Having begun brewing at the former Haffenreffer Brewery in Boston in 1988, Jim Koch's Boston Beer continued to also contract some of its production. In the mid-1990s Koch, a Cincinnati native, purchased the Hudepohl-Schoenling Brewery in that city, and later renamed it as the Samuel Adams Brewery. Coincidentally, his father had apprenticed in this brewery in the 1940s. In January 2005, Koch embarked on a major renovation and expansion of the brewery.

Across the continent in Chico, California, Ken Grossman bought out Paul Camusi, his partner at Sierra Nevada,

when Camusi retired in 1998. In the meantime, Grossman had traveled to Germany and brought back a traditional 100-barrel copper brew house, which became the heart of a new brewing facility. When the 1,500 percent growth of the 1990s outstripped capacity in 1997, Grossman commissioned the original coppersmiths to match new kettles to the originals, bringing the brewery's total capacity to almost 800,000 barrels per year.

The construction of a new brewery at Sierra Nevada gave the company the opportunity to also create a new taproom, restaurant and 350-seat "Big Room" complex that offered dining and live music, as well as its beer, including its flagship products and harder-to-find specialty drafts.

Of the nearly 1,500 breweries operating in the first decade of the twenty-first century, about a thousand were brewpubs, most producing fewer than a thousand barrels annually. Those who had grown above the 15,000-barrel annual production definition of a "microbrewery," now fit the new definition of "regional specialty" brewers. Since the turn of the century there have been about 50 breweries between the big five and the microbrewery threshold, and more than a dozen regional specialty brewers producing more than 100,000 barrels annually.

In addition to Boston Beer and Sierra Nevada, the upper tier of regional specialty brewers included the City Brewery of LaCrosse, Wisconsin, which expanded its annual output incredibly from 25,550 to 1,005,793 barrels between 2000 and 2005. The brewery itself was the former Heileman flagship brewery in LaCrosse, Wisconsin. Stroh had closed the plant after it acquired Heileman in 1996, and in 2000, the facility was acquired by a dozen local businessmen, who renamed it as the City Brewery. Historians will recall that this was the name given to the original brewery constructed on the site by John Gund and Gottlieb Heileman in 1858. The City Brewery initiated contract brewing, and scored a major piece of business when Pabst contracted with City to brew "Heileman's" Old Style — for which Pabst had acquired the trademark — at the birthplace of the brand. In April 2007, the City Brewery also began contract production of Samuel Adams products for the Boston Beer Company.

Also present in the upper tier of regional specialty brewers were nineteenth

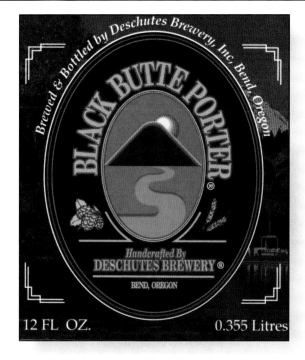

century veterans Latrobe Brewing of Latrobe, Pennsylvania, brewers of the famous Rolling Rock brand, and Genesee, which had renamed itself as High Falls Brewing in 1995.

Latrobe enjoyed a bit of a corporate parent odyssey during the "final consolidation" and its twenty-first century postscript. Purchased by Canada's Labatt Brewing Company in 1987, Latrobe was in turn acquired by the Belgian brewing conglomerate Interbrew (now InBev) when it absorbed Labatt in 1995. In 2006, InBev announced the sale of the Rolling Rock

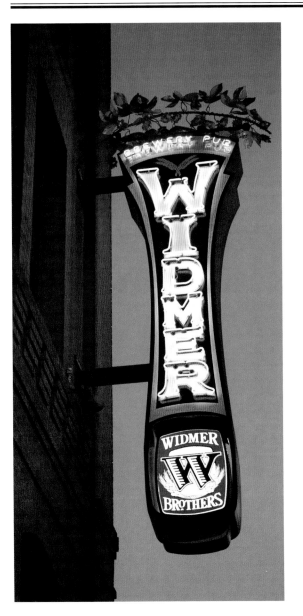

Left: **The marquee at the Widmer Brothers Brewery in Portland, Oregon.** *Below:* **The Widmer brew kettles.** *(Damian Conrad photo, courtesy of Trent Tokos, Widmer Brothers Brewing)*

brand — but not Latrobe Brewing — to Anheuser-Busch. Later the same year, InBev announced the sale of Latrobe and its Pennsylvania brewery to the City Brewing Company of LaCrosse. The final consolidation rolled on as Rolling Rock rolled toward St. Louis.

While the Rolling Rock brand reached the twenty-first century under someone else's corporate umbrella, another classic brand, the Rheingold brand from the Liebmann Brewery, was revived by an independent entity. Liebmann's original Brooklyn brewery was closed in 1976, and the New Jersey brewery closed the following year, but two decades later, Rheingold returned. In 1997, Mike Mitaro left his job as a marketing manager with Labatt United States to found the Rheingold Brewing Company and revive the legendary brand. The chairman of the new board would be Walter "Terry" Liebman (who spells his name with one "n"). A member of the original Liebmann family, Terry had worked in marketing at the original Liebmann Breweries until 1961, when he departed to work in the brokerage and investment banking industry. In turn the new Rheingold beer was brewed from an original Rheingold recipe at the F.X. Matt Brewing Company upstate in Utica, New York. Early in 2003, the Rheingold Brewing Company took the step that briefly revived one of the most important aspects of the Rheingold culture — they brought back Miss Rheingold. Whereas the original Miss Rheingolds were selected from a pool of models and actresses, the twenty-first century Miss Rheingolds would be chosen from among working bartenders and waitresses in the New York City area. Kate Duyn was crowned Miss Rheingold of 2003, and Dani Marco was selected as Miss Rheingold of 2004.

Other old brewery names included Pittsburgh Brewing, which dated back to the 1899 merger of 21 western Pennsylvania brewers; Leinenkugel Brewing, now owned by Miller, but reporting its data independently; the Spoetzl Brewery in Shiner, Texas; Matt Brewing in Utica, New York; and Joseph Huber Brewing of Monroe, Wisconsin, which is known for its Berghoff brand beers. Founded in 1845, Huber was originally known as the Blumer Brewery until it took the Huber name in 1947. The second oldest continually operating brewery in the United States, Huber was acquired in 2006 by Mountain Crest Brewing of Calgary, Alberta, Canada.

The former microbreweries in the upper tier of regional specialty brewers included New Belgium Brewing of Fort Collins, Colorado; Widmer Brothers in Portland, Oregon; Deschutes Brewing, of Bend, Oregon; Alaskan Brewing in Juneau; and Boulevard Brewing of Kansas City, Missouri, as well as two Seattle companies, Redhook and Pyramid Breweries. Founded in Kalama, Washington in 1984 as Hart Brewing, Pyramid subsequently

acquired Thomas Kemper Brewing and Portland Brewing. It is well known for its wheat beers, and for its five ale houses, located in Seattle, Portland and three cities in California.

New Belgium Brewing, well known for its Fat Tire Amber Ale, began in 1991 when home brewer Jeff Lebesch began operating commercially. On a trip across Belgium on a fat-tired bicycle, Lebesch was inspired by the imaginative beers that he discovered in Belgium — hence the brewery name and the brand name. The product line now has a half dozen brands, including seasonal beers. In the early days, it was a family business, with Lebesch's wife, Kim Jordan, part of the team. "Jeff would brew," she explains. "We would bottle together with some help from our son, Zack, then I would call accounts and deliver the beer. I'd get a lot of friendly ribbing pulling up in my station wagon full of beer next to these 16-bay Budweiser trucks."

In Portland, Oregon, the city that prides itself on having more breweries and brewpubs than any other American city, Widmer Brothers is the largest. Their Widmer's Hefeweizen has been Oregon's top-selling draught craft brew since the 1980s, and the brewery itself was named

Above: **Rob and Kurt Widmer.** *(Damian Conrad photo, courtesy of Widmer Brothers Brewing)*

"Mid-Size Brewery of the Year" at the Great American Beer Festival in 2002 and 2004. Across the state in Bend, Gary Fish's Deschutes Brewery expanded greatly from its roots with larger brewing facilities, and distribution into a dozen western states for its flagship products, including Black Butte Porter and Mirror Pond Pale Ale.

In Kansas City, Boulevard Brewing, who began marketing its beer in 1989, grew into the largest specialty brewer in the Midwest by the twenty-first century. Founded by John McDonald, Boulevard underwent small expansions in 1999 and 2003, and a major enlargement of operations in 2005 that gave it a 700,000-barrel annual capacity for its Pale Ale, Unfiltered Wheat Beer, Bully! Porter, Dry Stout and various seasonal beers.

By the turn of the century, the brewpub scene had matured considerably. While the archetypical brewpubs continued to flourish, the definition of brewpub had now been stretched to include full service restaurants that brew beer. This trend was indicative of the recognition that beer is just as important a complement to fine cuisine as wine. This evolved naturally because of the wide variety of beer styles that had become available — each one has a particular character that complements a particular type of food.

One of the original full-service brewery restaurants was Gordon Biersch, which was born in Palo Alto, California in 1988, and which evolved into a multi-site chain of brewery restaurants. The concept was created by a partnership between a brewer, Dan Gordon, and a chef, Dean Biersch. By the turn of the century, the company was serving patrons in a dozen locations across the United States.

Another chain that evolved from a single brewpub in the 1980s is McMenamin's Pubs & Breweries. By the early twenty-first century, it had expanded to an archipelago of over 50 brewpubs, microbreweries, music venues, historic hotels, theater pubs and more — nine are on the National Register of Historic Places. Centered in the Portland, Oregon metropolitan area, McMenamin's has many other locations in Oregon and Washington. According to the Association of Brewers, as of 2003 it is the third largest brewpub chain in the United States, serving approximately 20,000 barrels annually. Unlike most chains, brewmasters at McMenamin's locations are encouraged through an annual intra-company competition, to experiment with new beers.

A number of other chains of brewery restaurants began to come on the scene around the turn of the century, including the Tampa-based Hops Restaurant Brewery chain, B.J.'s Restaurants and the Rock Bottom Restaurants of Louisville, Colorado.

The notion of the twenty-first century as the era in which the craft brewing segment truly came into its own is certainly born out by the data. According to the Brewers Association of Boulder, Colorado, craft beer industry sales grew 31.5 percent in one 36 month period early in the century. The total craft beer industry annual dollar volume approached five billion dollars. In addition to the 50 regional specialty breweries, there were more than 350 microbreweries and nearly a thousand brewpubs in operation in the United States. The number of new microbrewery openings was outpacing microbrewery closings by three to one.

Of course not all United States breweries are in North America. Across the Pacific in Hawaii, the American brewing tradition goes back to the Honolulu Brewing Company, started in 1898, and the Hawaii Brewing Company (also in Honolulu) that was formed in 1934. The latter became famous for its Primo brand that

Above: Jeff Lebesch and Kim Jordan of New Belgium Brewing. *Left:* Their popular Fat Tire Amber. *Opposite:* Their brewery in Fort Collins. *(Photos courtesy of Adrian Matthew, New Belgium Brewing)*

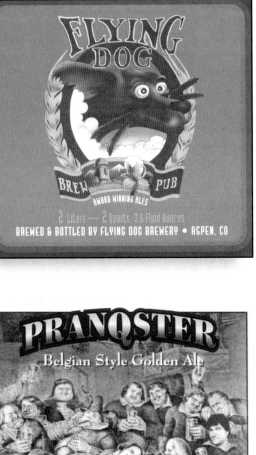

Clockwise from above: **Classic craft brewers from around the West include Lagunitas Brewing in Petaluma, California; the Flying Dog Brewery in Aspen, Colorado; Rogue Ales in Newport, Oregon; and North Coast Brewing in Fort Bragg, California. North Coast's Pranqster is possibly the best Belgian style ale brewed in the United States.** *(Courtesy of the breweries)*

dominated the Hawaiian market up until Schlitz bought the company in 1964. Primo faded quickly when Schlitz moved production to the mainland in the 1970s, and the brand eventually disappeared. Through the 1980s and 1990s, a number of microbreweries came and went, including Koolau on the island of Oahu and Pacific on Maui. Today, several brewery restaurants exist in the islands, including the Gordon Biersch operation in Honolulu and Waimea Brewing on the island of

Kauai, which is the westernmost brewpub in the world.

The microbrewery scene in Hawaii is best exemplified by the Kona Brewing Company on the Big Island of Hawaii, which has been the leading Hawaiian micro since 1996. Started in the spring of 1994 by the father and son team of Cameron Healy and Spoon Khalsa, Kona now sells more craft beer than any other micro in the state, and is four times larger than any other Hawaiian brewery. Kona Brewing's first bottling was in February 1995 and Pacific Golden Ale (now called Big Wave Golden Ale) and Fire Rock Pale Ale were introduced in bottles and kegs. Longboard Island Lager was added to the lineup three years later. Approximately ten other styles of beer are brewed on a regular basis and served at Kona Brewing's pubs in Kona and on Oahu, with a select few being served at some restaurants. Limited release beers are also distributed throughout the western United States.

The success of the companies from Kona Brewing to Boston Beer, or from Sierra Nevada to New Belgium, is indicative of the success of the craft beer renaissance that began back in the early 1980s and which had flourished in the twenty-first century.

"Craft beer volume growth far exceeded that of large brewers, wine and spirits in 2005," said Paul Gatza, Director of the Brewers Association of Boulder, Colorado. "And even though imported beer grew nicely in 2005, craft beer grew at a faster rate."

As *Modern Brewery Age* wrote in 2006, "Beer shipments were down 1.2 percent in 2005, but this was not a reflection on every domestic player. Yuengling, Boston Beer and Sierra Nevada sold more beer, Anheuser-Busch, Miller and Coors sold less. . . . Indeed, high-end beer thrived in 2005. Craft brewers were up nine percent [in 2005 and 12 percent in 2006], according to the Brewers Association, and imports climbed 7.2 percent . . . In years past, Anheuser-Busch would add a couple of million barrels without breathing hard, but this time they dropped 1.9 million. . . Ephemeral or not, craft and import growth has put the big brewers in the shade."

Industry veteran and *Modern Brewery Age* columnist Bob Wilson added that

"Many of today's consumers are drinking something other than lagers. The major brewers are selling just vanilla, while the 21-34 year-olds are looking for 28 flavors. This is one of the reasons the craft brewers are doing well."

Among the other reasons were the strong regional identities that had been forged by the craft brew-

Below: Brewing ephemera from Hawaii includes contemporary six-packs from Kona Brewing; a label from the late Pacific Brewing on Maui; and a photo of the Gordon Biersch brewery restaurant in Honolulu. *(Images courtesy of the breweries)*

Above: The new brewhouse at Boulevard Brewing Company in Kansas City. Founded in 1989, Boulevard is the largest specialty brewer in the Midwest.
Right: Unfiltered Wheat Beer from Boulevard Brewing. *(Images courtesy of Becca Alexander, Boulevard Brewing)*

Opposite: The brewhouse at Anchor Brewing in San Francisco. *(Terry McCarthy photo via Anchor Brewing)*

ers since the 1980s, and the ever-growing acceptance of beer as part of all phases of American life and culture.

In the word of the great United States Brewers Foundation institutional advertising campaign from a half century before, consumers had come to celebrate the notion that "beer belongs."

The words of Stanley Baron, writing in *Brewed in America* in 1962, were both profound and prophetic. "Curiously, one of the means by which beer sales have been pushed to record levels in recent times has been the successful campaign to bring beer back to its original social position: a universal beverage," wrote Baron. "It is no longer the workingman's drink, it is no longer a German drink, it is no longer exclusively a man's drink. Most of these temporary labels have been removed by one method or another, and the acceptance of beer is closer than ever to where it was at the beginning. The kettle in the kitchen has given way to the tremendous factory covering several city blocks, but the drink in the glass fills the same purpose it always has."

In Baron's time, the "kettle in the kitchen" had indeed given way to "the tremendous factory," but since the 1980s, the craft brewer has brought beer full circle. Indeed, many of the patriarchs of the craft brew revolution started out as home brewers, literally with kettles in their kitchens.

Today, the diversity and complexity of beers that fill the glasses, and the breweries that make those beers, provides the beer drinker with many opportunities for enjoyment. "They are looking for richer and more interesting lives," Fritz Maytag said of these consumers. "I find it very satisfying to put meaning into products."

It is only right that this should happen in America, where founding fathers from George Washington to Jefferson brewed beer, praised its qualities and heartily supported American brewers. Both men realized that a diverse industry is a healthy industry. Trends in the market that have been ongoing since the last decade of the twentieth century indicate that this will both continue and flourish in the future.

GLOSSARY

Adjunct: The Siebel Institute of Technology, America's oldest brewing school, defines an adjunct as unmalted grain, sugars or syrups used in brewing.

Admiral: An English bittering hop used in some English ales.

Ahtanum: An American aroma hop developed by Yakima Chief Ranches, similar to Cascade.

Ale: A top-fermented beer that was brewed in England as early as the seventh century and made with hops after the sixteenth century. It is fermented at temperatures ranging between 55 degrees F and 70 degrees F (13 degrees C and 21 degrees C), warmer than those used to ferment lager. It is the primary beer type in England and among North American microbreweries, but less common elsewhere. Subtypes include pale ale (which is actually much more amber than pale lagers), brown ale and India pale ale, a beer developed in the nineteenth century by English brewers for export to the British Empire.

Alpha Acid: This is the bitter hop resin responsible for bitterness of beer. Measured as a percentage of the total weight of the hop cone. The content of alpha acid is measured in Alpha Acid Units (AAU), the percentage of alpha acid multiplied by the weight in ounces of a sample. An ounce of hops with an alpha content of 1 percent contains 1 AAU, or .01 ounce of alpha acid. (See beta acid)

Altbier: The German equivalent of English or American "ale," literally a beer made in the "old" way (pre-nineteenth century) with top-fermenting yeast. It is indigenous to Dusseldorf, Germany and environs. Virtually unknown in the United States after Prohibition, it was reintroduced by several American several microbreweries in the 1980s.

Amarillo (VGX001): A popular American mid-range alpha acid content hop developed by Virgil Gamache Farms in late 20th century.

Balling scale: A measurement developed by Karl Balling that is used mainly in the brewing industry to indicate the concentration of sucrose in a solution at 17.5 degrees C.

Barley Wine: In Britain, ales with alcohol contents approaching that of wine (up to and surpassing 10 percent by volume) are called barley wines.

Barrel: The Siebel Institute of Technology, America's oldest brewing school, defines it as a generic name for a cask or keg, a container for transporting draft beer, or a unit of liquid volume measure. As the latter, a United States beer barrel equals 31 US gallons, a Canadian beer barrel equals 25 Imperial gallons and a British beer barrel equals 36 Imperial gallons, or 1.2 hectoliters.

Beer: A general term for all fermented malt beverages flavored with hops. The term embraces ale, lager, porter, stout and all other types discussed herein. Ingredients include malted cereal grains (especially, but not limited to, barley), hops, yeast and water, although early English beers were unhopped. Subtypes are classified by whether they are made with top-fermenting yeast (ale, porter, stout, wheat beer) or bottom-fermenting yeast (lager, bock beer, malt liquor). Generally, top-fermented beers are darker, ranging from a translucent copper to opaque brown, while bottom-fermented beers range from amber to pale yellow. Because of their English heritage, top-fermented beers are usually drunk at room temperature, while bottom-fermented beers are served cold.

Beta Acid: This is bitter hop resin that is harsher in flavor than alpha acid but almost insoluble at normal wort pH values. (See alpha acid)

Bier: The German, Dutch and Flemish word for beer.

Biére: The French word for beer.

Birra: The Italian word for beer.

Bitter: A full-bodied, highly hopped ale (hence the name) that is extremely popular in England but less so elsewhere. Bitter (or bitter ale) is similar in color to other ales, but it lacks carbonation and has a slightly higher alcohol content. A noun used in England to identify highly-hopped ale. Originally it was probably short for bitter ale. The little-used antonym is "mild," also a noun, which implies a lightly hopped English ale.

Bock Beer: A bottom-fermented beer that is darker than lager and which has a relatively higher alcohol content, usually in the six percent range. Bock originated in Germany and most German brewers still brew it as a special supplement to their principal product line. Prior to World War II, many American brewers produced a bock beer each spring, but the advent of national marketing after the war largely eliminated the practice of brewing seasonal beers. In the 1980s, several breweries began to reintroduce bock beer. The male goat (bock in German) is the traditional symbol of bock beer. Subtypes include doppelbock, a bock especially high in alcohol, and maibock, a bock marketed in conjunction with May festivals.

Brasserie: The French word for brewery, also a term for a small café.

Bräuerei: The German word for brewery.

Brewer's Gold: A British bittering hop developed in 1934 from Bullion. Occasionally used as aroma variety with noble hops.

Breweriana: Americans have a peculiar interest in(some would say "obsession with") the artifacts of their civilization. This manifests itself particularly in collecting. Americans are inveterate collectors. In the case of our American brewing heritage, the object of the collector is called "breweriana." This general topic includes anything related to brewing, but is centers especially on objects related to the marketing and packaging of beer. Breweriana aficionados typically collect branded artifacts that relate to a specific favorite brewery or a specific product. Foremost on the list are labels, bottles, cans and coasters. More serious collectors search for such things as tap handles, promotional novelties and signs. Lighted signs, including neon and the famous Hamm's and Olympia "waterfall" signs are among the most highly sought. Breweriana fans also collect ephemera, such as magazine advertising and souvenir booklets that were given away free at brewery tours through the years. As with other collectors, many breweriana lovers have organized themselves into clubs. Some of the most notable are the American Breweriana Association, which publishes the American Breweriana Journal, as well as the National Association Breweriana Advertising and Beer Can Collectors of America. Many breweries, especially fondly-remembered breweries from the past, have active fan clubs and historical societies.

Brewing: Generically, the entire beer-making process, but technically only that part of the process during which the beer wort is cooked in a brew kettle and during which time the hops are added. Following the brewing, beer is fermented. (see fermentation.)

Above: A beer for dad. (*Library of Congress*)

Brewpub: A pub or tavern that brews its own beer on the premises. They existed in Boston in 1639, and were common from then through the nineteenth century. With the enactment of the 18th Amendment in 1920, they disappeared completely for six decades. Until the 1980s, as a holdover from Prohibition laws, it was illegal in most states and Canadian provinces to both brew beer and sell it directly to the public on the same site. Subsequent changes in local laws have rescinded these outdated restrictions and have made it possible for brewpubs to become more widespread. A brewpub differs from a microbrewery in that its primary market is under its own roof. Some brewpubs bottle their beers for sale to patrons and for wholesale to retailers, while some microbreweries also operate brewpubs, so the distinction between the two is somewhat blurred. Both, however, share a commitment to their own unique beers, and most brewpublicans entered their trade out of a love for brewing and an interest in distinctive beer styles. As defined by the Brewers Association, brewpub is a restaurant-brewery that sells 25 percent or more of its beer on site. The beer is brewed primarily for sale in the restaurant and bar. The beer is often dispensed directly from the brewery's storage tanks. Where allowed by law, brewpubs often sell beer "to go" and/or distribute to off site accounts.

Brouwerij: The Dutch and Flemish word for brewery.

Cascade: A very successful and well-established American aroma hop developed by Oregon State University's breeding program in 1956 from Fuggles and Russian Serebrianker hops, but not released for cultivation until 1972.

Cask-conditioning: Secondary fermentation and maturation in the cask at the point of sale. The process creates light carbonation.

Centennial: An American aroma-type variety bred in 1974 and released in 1990, it is similar to Cascade and Chinook.

Cerveceria: The Spanish word for brewery.

Cerveja: The Portuguese word for beer.

Cerveza: The Spanish word for beer.

Challenger: An English hop with fresh pine notes, it was introduced in 1972.

Chinook: An American cross between Petham Goldings hops and a USDA-selected male hops. Typical American citric pine hop with notable grapefruit and pineapple flavors.

Columbus: A high yielding, high alpha acid American bittering hop, it is also known by the trade name Tomahawk.

Contract Brewing Company: As defined by the Brewers Association, this a business that hires another brewery to produce its beer. It can also be a brewery that hires another brewery to produce additional beer. The contract brewing company handles marketing, sales, and distribution of its beer, while generally leaving the brewing and packaging to its producer-brewery (which, confusingly, is also sometimes referred to as a contract brewery).

Craft beer: As defined by the Brewers Association, craft beers are produced with 100 percent barley or wheat malt or use other fermentable ingredients that enhance (rather than lighten) flavor. Craft beers only come from craft brewers.

Craft brewer: As defined by the Brewers Association, an American craft brewer is small, independent and traditional. Craft beer comes only from a craft brewer.

Cream Ale: A blend of ale and lager invented in the early twentieth century by American brewers.

Crystal: An aromatic American triploid hop variety developed in 1993 from Hallertau, Cascade, and others.

Diat: A German word for lager low in carbohydrates originally developed for diabetic people. It is not a "diet" or low-calorie beer.

Doppelbock: A German word literally meaning "double bock." Although it is not nearly twice as strong as bock, it is typically the highest alcohol (over seven percent by volume) beer style brewed in Germany but lower in alcohol than English Barley Wine. In naming practice, German doppelbocks are given names ending in "ator," such as Animator, Celebrator, Kulminator, Maximator, Optimator, Salvator, and Triumphator.

Draft (Draught) Beer: A term which literally means beer that is drawn from a keg rather than packaged in bottles or cans. Designed for immediate use, draft beer is not pasteurized and hence must be kept cold to prevent the loss of its fresh taste. Draft beer is generally better than packaged beer when fresh but not so as it ages. Some brewers sell unpasteurized draft-style beer in cans and bottles, which must be shipped in refrigerated containers.

Dry Beer: The term was adopted in the 1980s for pale lagers in which all the fermentable sugars from the original malt have been converted to alcohol. In order to conclude the process with a beer of acceptable alcohol content (roughly 3.2 percent by weight), a brewer must start with less malt. Hence, dry beer has a low original gravity and will have very little flavor unless it is more heavily hopped than typical beers. The process is similar to that used to produce light beer, and the results are very similar. In fact, most American mass market lagers, including light and dry beers, are very similar in taste. Beer in which all fermentable sugars are fermented was developed in Germany and Switzerland in the 1970s as diat beer, a beer designed for diabetic people.

Dry-hopping: The addition of dry hops to fermenting or aging beer to increase its hop character or aroma.

Dunkel (Dunkles): A German adjective used to describe a dark lager, usually in the sweeter Munich style.

Eisbock: A German term that originated in Dortmund and applied to especially flavorful and powerful light-colored lagers.

Eroica: A strongly flavored bittering hop used in wheat beers.

ESB (Extra Special Bitter): A term that originated in England for describing a brewer's best highly-hopped bitter ale.

Export: This style evolved when the brewers in Dortmund, Germany, began transporting beer to other markets across the continent. In order to withstand the rigors of travel, they produced a beer that was well hopped and slightly higher in alcohol. As such, the Dortmund lager as a style is known as "export." Dortmunder lagers are traditionally full-bodied but not quite as sweet as the beers of Munich, though not as dry as a true Pilsner. Beers identified as such are not necessarily brewed specifically to be exported, although they often are.

Fermentation: The process by which yeast turns the sugars present in malted grains into alcohol and carbon dioxide.

First Gold: An English dwarf hop that is a cross-pollination of Whitbread Goldings variety and a dwarf male. It is like a spicier Goldings, with a higher alpha acid content and slightly richer bitterness.

Above: **The largest bottle of beer in Vincennes, Indiana, 1940.** (*Library of Congress*)

Fuggles: The main English hop, developed in the late nineteenth century. Considered by some to be less refined than Goldings, others prefer its juicier, woodier character.

Galena: An American bittering hop developed from Brewer's Gold by open pollination in Idaho. Has a moderate bitterness despite its high alpha acid content content.

Glacier: A low-cohumulone American Fuggles hop descendant. Mild bittering and soft, fruity character with hints of apricot and pear.

Goldings: The traditional and very popular English aroma hop. Developed in 1790, it has a soft, earthy, vaguely farm-like aroma. Widely cultivated. Called East Kent Goldings if grown in East Kent, Kent Goldings if grown in mid-Kent, and Goldings if grown elsewhere.

Greenburg: An American Hop from southern Idaho that has a fruity flavor with a touch of woody flavors, it is used mainly in microbrews.

Gueuze: Blended Belgian lambic beers not containing fruits.

Hallertau: The original German lager hop. Due to susceptibility to disease, it was largely replaced by Hersbrucker in the 1970s and 1980s.

Hell (Helles): An adjective used in Germany to describe lager that is pale in color.

Herald: An English aroma and bittering hop, which is related to the Pioneer.

Hersbrucker: A noble hop used in German pale lagers. Noted for grass and hay aroma.

Hops: The dried blossom of the female hop plant which is a climbing herb (*Humulus lupulus*) native to temperate regions of the Northern Hemisphere and cultivated in Europe, the United Kingdom and the United States. Belonging to the mulberry family, the hop's leaves and flowers are characterized by a bitter taste and aroma. It has been used since the ninth century as the principal flavoring and seasoning agent in brewing, although it had been prized before that for its medicinal properties. In addition to its aromatic resins, the hop also contains tannin which helps to clarify beer. Different strains of hops have different properties and much of the brewmaster's art is in knowing how to use these properties. For example, one strain may be particularly bitter to the taste without being very aromatic, while another strain might be just the opposite. The brewmaster will blend the two in various combinations just as a chef will experiment with various seasonings before set-

tling on just the right combination for a particular recipe. Hops also serve as a natural preservative.

Horizon: An American high alpha acid content hop made in Oregon in 1970 from Nugget. Soft bitterness.

Ice Beer: Developed and patented by Labatt in Canada, ice beer is a pale lager which is quickly chilled to sub-freezing temperatures after brewing but before final fermentation. The result is the formation of ice crystals in the beer, which are removed to produce a beer with roughly twice the alcohol content of typical mass market lagers.

India Pale Ale (IPA): A type of highly hopped, but light-colored, ale developed in England in the late eighteenth century, IPA was designed specifically to not deteriorate in quality during the long voyage to India.

International Bitterness Unit (IBU): Brewers can and actually do measure bitterness in their beer using the IBU scale. An IBU is one part per million of isohumulone. The higher number, the greater the bitterness. Bland, mass market lagers might be as low as 5, while the most bitter of English ales may be as high as 80.

Keller: A German-style of packaged, unfiltered lager that emulates vom fass (on draft) beer. A keller is also a German "beer cellar."

Kräusening (Kraeusening): The process of instigating a secondary fermentation to produce additional carbon dioxide in a beer. Some brewers will first ferment their beer in open containers where alcohol is produced and retained, but the carbon dioxide escapes. The second fermentation, or kraeusening, then takes place in closed containers after a first fermentation (whether that first fermentation took place in open or closed containers) and is used to produce natural carbonation or sparkle in the beer.

Kriek: A Belgian lambic flavored with cherries, it is the most popular of the fruit lambics.

Lager: This beer style accounts for well over 90 percent of the beer brewed and marketed in the world (outside England). Specifically, it is a clear, pale beer fermented with bottom-fermenting yeast at nearly freezing temperatures. The fermentation period is longer than that for ale and hence the name, which is German meaning "to store." Lager had its origins in the heart of central Europe in an area that the author likes to call the Golden Triangle. This triangle is so named because of the golden color of lager itself and because of the success that brewers had with this product when it was first developed for widespread commercial sale in the early to middle nineteenth century. The corners of the Triangle lie in Munich, Prague and Vienna, the capitals, respectively, of Bavaria (a state of the German Federal Republic), Bohemia (Czech Republic) and Austria.

Lambic: A style of beer fermented with special strains of wild yeast indigenous only to Belgium's Senne Valley. One of the world's most unique native beer styles.

Lauter Tun: The vessel used in brewing between the mash tun and the brew kettle. It separates the barley husks from the clear liquid wort. The barley husks themselves help provide a natural filter bed through which the wort is strained.

Lauter: To run the wort from the mash tun. From the German word to clarify. A lauter tun is a separate vessel to do this job. It uses a system of sharp rakes to achieve a very intensive extraction of malt sugars.

Light Beer: The term was long used by American brewers in advertising, but as a style, it was introduced in the mid-1970s by

nearly every major brewer in the United States and Canada, light beers are by definition reduced-calorie lagers or ales. They also have a slightly lower alcohol content than comparable lagers or ales.

Magnum: A bittering/aroma type hop cultivar, bred in 1980 at Huell, the German Hop Research Institute, from the American variety Galena and the German male.

Maibock: A bock beer brewed for release in May.

Malt Liquor: A bottom-fermented beer, it has a malty taste more closely related to top-fermented ale than to lager which is bottom-fermented. Malt liquor has a much higher alcohol content (5.6 to 6.5 percent) than lager. It is a government-imposed term used to identify beer with an alcohol content above five percent. It is not actually a true beer type as the term may be used with ales or lagers. Some larger American brewers produce very pale high-alcohol lagers and call them malt liquors.

Malting: The process by which barley kernels are moistened and germinated, producing a "green malt" which is then dried. This renders the starches present in the kernel soluble. If pale beers are to be produced, the malt is sim-

Above: **A classic national brand, a classic tavern sign, circa 1930s.** (*Library of Congress*)

ply dried. If dark beers are to be produced, the malt is roasted until it is dark brown. The malt is then subjected to mashing.

Märzen: Originally this German term was used to describe a reddish lager brewed in March and set aside for summer. The style is now brewed for autumn consumption, particularly in connection with Oktoberfest.

Mash Tun: A tank where grist is soaked in water and heated in order to convert the starch to sugar and extract the sugars and other solubles from the grist.

Mash: The substance that is produced by mashing.

Mashing: The process by which barley malt is mixed with water and cooked to turn soluble starch into fermentable sugar. Other cereal grains, such as corn and rice, many also be added (rice contributes to a paler end product beer). After mashing in a mash tun, the mash is filtered through a lauter tun, whereupon it becomes known as wort.

Microbrewery: As defined by the Brewers Association, this a brewery that produces less than 15,000 barrels (17,600 hectoliters) of beer per year with 75 percent or more of its beer

sales off site. Microbreweries sell to the public by one or more of the following methods: the traditional three-tier system (brewer to wholesaler to retailer to consumer); the two-tier system (brewer acting as wholesaler to retailer to consumer); and, directly to the consumer through carryouts and/or on-site taproom or restaurant sales.

Millennium: A bittering hop variety, bred from Nugget and with similar characteristics.

Mount Hood: A soft American hop variety developed from Hallertau, it is frequently used in styles that require only a subtle hop aroma.

Near Beer: Nonalcoholic beer which originated during the Prohibition era in the United States and which is still in production.

Newport: A recently developed American high-alpha acid content bittering hop.

Noble hops: Hop varieties that are the genetic basis for most of the other hop varieties used in the world today. In fact, some of the greatest beer styles only use these hop strains.

Northdown: A dual-purpose hop developed in England in 1970s, with a Northern Brewer-like bitterness, and soft aroma.

Northern Brewer: A hop developed in England in 1934 from a cross between a female hop of wild American parentage and an English male. Grown in Europe and America as a dual-purpose hop, but the aroma is mellow, so is mainly used for bittering in combination with other hops.

Nugget: A variety of bittering hop.

Pacific Gem: A high alpha acid content bittering hop from New Zealand. Most are organic and have a pleasant woody flavor and berry aroma.

Palisade: A fairly recent American hop that is a cross of Tettnager and open pollination resulting in a moderate alpha acid content hop with good aroma characteristics.

Pasteurization: Though this term has come to mean the heating of a substance to kill harmful bacteria, the process was originally proposed by Louis Pasteur as a means of killing yeast to end fermentation and hence end the creation of alcohol and carbon dioxide (carbonation). Unpasteurized beers are no less sanitary than pasteurized beers.

Perle: A German dual-purpose hop, with floral, spicy aroma. Often used in combination with other hops.

Pils: A European synonym for Pilseners.

Pilsener or Pilsner: A pale bottom-fermented lager beer originally associated with the city of Pilsen, Bohemia (Czech Republic) where it was first brewed in the early nineteenth century. The term is often used interchangeably with the term lager, although pilsners are technically the palest of lagers. Pilsners are the most widely known and widely imitated lager type. The Plzensky Prazdroj brewery in Pilsen brews Pilsner Urquell ("Pilsner from the original source"), which is considered the definitive pilsner, although the term has become generic.

Pioneer: An English hop that is a sister of Herald, it provides a clean, soft and rounded bitterness with a recognizable English aroma.

Plato (degrees of): Plato explains the specific gravity as the weight of extract in a 100 gram solution at 64 degrees F (17.5 degrees C). It is a refinement of the Balling scale.

Porter: A dark, sweet beer brewed with top-fermenting (ale type) yeast that was developed in London in the late eighteenth century and revived by American microbrewers in the late twentieth century. It took its name from the city's porters who had taken an immediate fancy to it. Similar to but sweeter than stout, it is a dark beer of moderate strength (alcohol, five to seven percent by volume), made with roasted unmalted barley.

Pride of Ringwood: A famous Australian hop, it was first used in 1965 when it was the highest alpha acid hop in the world. Used extensively in Australian pale ales and lagers.

Progress: A high alpha acid content English hop developed in the 1960s as a replacement for Fuggles. It is often used with Goldings.

Prohibition: The process by which a government prohibits its citizens from buying or possessing alcoholic beverages. Specifically, the Prohibition refers to the period between the effective date of the 18th Amendment to the US Constitution (January 16, 1920) and its repeal by the 21st Amendment. Repeal took effect on 5 December 1933, although it passed Congress in February and the sale of beer was permitted after April 7, 1933.

Rauchbier: A lager with a wonderfully smoky flavor which uses malted grain that has been roasted over a very smoky beechwood fire.

Indigenous to the Bamberg area in southern Germany, rauchbier means literally "smoked beer." As such, the grain is not only roasted to a dark color, but it takes on a distinctive smoky flavor as well. Smoked beer, which is rare outside of Germany, is generally served with meals including smoked or barbecued meats, rye bread and certain sharp cheeses.

Regional Brewery: As defined by the Brewers Association, this a brewery with an annual beer production of between 15,000 and 2 million barrels. These are also called "regional specialty" breweries when distinguished from "regional craft" breweries.

Regional Craft Brewery: As defined by the Brewers Association, this is an independent regional brewery who has either an all malt flagship or has at least 50 percent of its volume in either all malt beers or in beers which use adjuncts to enhance rather than lighten flavor.

Reinheitsgebot: This "Purity Law" originating in Bavaria in 1516 and now applied to all German brewers making beer for consumption in their own country. It requires that only malted grains, hops, yeast and water may be used in the brewing. This regulation originated in the city of Ingolstadt in the duchy of Bavaria on April 23, 1516, although first put forward in

Above: **A brew kettle at the late Tivoli Union Brewery in Denver.** (*Library of Congress*)

1487, concerning standards for the sale and composition of beer. In the original text, the only ingredients that could be used in the production of beer were water, barley, and hops. The Reinheitsgebot is no longer part of German law: it has been replaced by the Provisional German Beer Law (Vorlaufiges Deutsches Biergesetz (Provisional German Beer-law of 1993), which allows constituent components prohibited in the Reinheitsgebot, such as wheat malt and cane sugar, but which no longer allows unmalted barley.

Saaz: A noble hop used extensively in Bohemia, and found in most Czech pale lagers. Soft, yet pleasing in aroma and bitterness.

Sake: A fermented beverage that is a cousin to the family of fermented beverages we call beer. Sake originated in Japan where it is an important national drink. Several sake breweries have existed in both California and Hawaii over the years, but the only remaining American commercial sake brewery is in Hawaii. Sake is brewed from unmalted rice and is not hopped. The resulting substance is clear and has a 14 to 16 percent alcohol content. In contrast to beer, which is drunk either chilled or at room temperature, sake is warmed before drinking.

Santiam: An American floral aroma hop with mid-range alpha acid content, its pedigree includes Tettnang, Hallertau and Cascade.

Satus: A bittering hop cultivar of recent origin.

Select: A German disease-resistant Hallertau and Spalt pale lager hop variety developed in early 1990s.

Simcoe: An American high alpha acid content hop variety released in 2000. Distinctive passion fruit flavor and aroma where Simcoe hops are utilized late in the boil.

Spalt: The traditional German noble hop, with a delicate, spicy aroma.

Specific gravity (relative density): The ratio of the mass of a solid or liquid to the mass of an equal volume of distilled water at 4 degrees C (39.2 degrees F) or of a gas to an equal volume of air or hydrogen under prescribed conditions of temperature and pressure.

Steam Beer: A term that seems to have been a nickname for beer brewed on the West Coast of America under primitive conditions and without ice. The brewing methods of those days are a mystery and, although there are many theories, no one can say with certainty why the

word "steam" came to be associated with beer. For many decades Anchor Brewing Company of San Francisco alone has used this quaint name for its unique beer. In modern times, "Steam" has become a trademark of Anchor Brewing for its Anchor Steam Beer.

Sterling: An American floral hop released in 1998, it is a cross between Saaz and Mount Hood in character but easier to grow.

Stout: A dark, dense beer produced with top-fermenting (ale type) yeast. Stout is the prominent beer type in Ireland and is widely available in England. Also brewed occasionally by microbreweries in the United States, it is not nearly so popular in continental Europe. Guinness, brewed in Dublin, is the definitive stout of the Irish type. It is also brewed under license in many places throughout the world. English brewers, such as Samuel Smith in Tadcaster, also produce oatmeal stout in which oats are used along with barley malt.

Strisselspalt: A French aroma hop from Alsace, used mostly in pale lagers, it is similar to Herbrucker.

Styrian Goldings: A Slovenian variant of Fuggles hops, used in English ales and Belgian strong ales amongst others.

Target: An earthy English mid-to-high alpha acid content hop bred from Kent Goldings.

Tesguino: A type of corn beer produced by the Indians of Mexico and the American Southwest prior to their contact with Europeans.

Tettnang: A noble German dual use hop used in European pale lagers, sometimes with Hallertau. Soft bitterness.

Tradition: A hop variety bred in 1991 from Hallertau hops by the Hull Hop Research Institute in Germany for resistance to disease. It is said to be "grassy" like Hallertau, but easier to grow.

Ultra: A triploid aroma-type hop cultivar, originated in 1983 from a cross between the colchicine-induced tetraploid Hallertau and the diploid Saaz-derived male genotype. Ultra is related to Mount Hood, Liberty and Crystal.

Vanguard: An American aroma hop cross-developed from Hallertau in 1982.

Warrior: A recent American bittering hop variety, popular with growers and brewers.

Weissbier: A German word literally meaning beer that is white (weiss), but actually implying a style of pale-colored, top- fermented beer made with about half wheat malt. Various styles are typical of places within Germany such as Bavarian or Berlin. A hefeweiss or hefeweizen beer is a weissbier in which yeast (in German, hefe) sediment remains in suspension in the beer. Weissbier is also known as weizenbier, but should not be confused with wiesenbier, which is a festival beer that may or may not contain wheat malt.

Wheat Beer: Beer, by definition, is a beverage derived from malted barley. Other grains, such as rice and cornmeal, are often used in less expensive, mass market brands as a cheaper source of starch, but this practice is frowned upon by discriminating brewers and consumers. Exceptions are made in the case of oats in English oatmeal stout and with wheat in American wheat beer, German weissbier and Flemish witbier. Both the German and Flemish terms are literally translated as meaning "white" beer. This is a reference to the light color of the beer and the fact that it usually has yeast particles in suspension and hence it is cloudy, translucent and lighter in appearance than if it were transparent. In Germany, weissbiers that are cloudy are identified with the prefix "hefe" (yeast) as "hefeweizen" or "hefeweiss" beers. (See Weissbier and Witbier.)

Willamette: A popular American development in 1976 of the English Fuggle. Mild aroma hop, with a fruity character.

Witbier/Biére Blanche: Flemish/French literally meaning white (wit/blanche) beer. It is brewed using over half wheat malt. A cousin to German weissbier, witbier is indigenous to the northern, Flemish-speaking areas of Belgium.

Wort: An oatmeal-like substance consisting of water and mashed barley in which soluble starch has been turned into fermentable sugar during the mashing process. The wort is cooked, or brewed, in the brew kettle for more than an hour and for as much as a day, during which time hops are added to season the wort. After brewing, the hopped wort is filtered and fermented to produce beer.

Yeast: The enzyme-producing one-celled fungi of the genus Saccharomyces that is added to wort before the fermentation process for the purpose of turning fermentable sugar into alcohol and carbon dioxide.

Zeus: American aromatic high alpha acid content hops with noticeable bitterness, it is similar to Columbus.

Above: **The fermenters at Gunther Brewing in Baltimore, 1933.** (*Library of Congress*)

APPENDICES

ANNUAL OUTPUT OF THE UNITED STATES BREWING INDUSTRY
(In 31-gallon barrels)

1860	3,812,346
1870	6,574,617
1880	13,347,111
1890	27,561,944
1900	39,471,593
1910	59,552,299
1914	66,189,473*
1920	9,231,280**
1930	3,681,183**
1933	11,059,071***
1934	37,678,313****
1940	54,891,737
1950	88,807,075
1960	94,547,867
1970	134,653,881
1980	188,373,657
1990	203,658,410
2000	199,173,709
2005	194,347,826

*	Pre-Prohibition Peak Year
**	Near Beer Only
***	The Year that Prohibition was Repealed
****	The first full year after Prohibition

Source: Brewer's Almanac.

TOTAL UNITED STATES MARKET SHARE CONTROLLED BY THE TOP FIVE AMERICAN BREWING COMPANIES

1950:	24 percent
1960:	32 percent
1970:	49 percent
1980:	75 percent
1990:	91 percent
2000:	95 percent

PROPORTION OF AMERICAN BEER SOLD ON DRAFT (VERSUS IN CANS OR BOTTLES) IN SELECTED YEARS:

1934	75 percent
1935	70 percent
1937	56 percent
1945	36 percent
1946	33.4 percent
1950	28.2 percent
1960	19.3 percent
1970	14.1 percent
1980	12.1 percent
1990	11.1 percent
2000	9.3 percent
2002	9.1 percent
2005	9.3 percent

THE EVOLUTION OF AMERICA'S TOP BREWING COMPANIES
(in Millions of Barrels sold in the US Market)

1950: The Top Five Brewing Companies	Annual Output	Share of Total
1. Schlitz	5.1	6 percent
2. Anheuser-Busch	4.9	6 percent
3. Ballantine	4.4	5 percent
4. Pabst	3.4	4 percent
5. Schaefer	2.8	3 percent

1960: The Top Five Brewing Companies		
1. Anheuser-Busch	8.5	10 percent
2. Schlitz	5.7	6 percent
3. Falstaff	4.9	6 percent
4. Carling	4.8	5 percent
5. Pabst	4.7	5 percent

1970: The Top Five Brewing Companies		
1. Anheuser-Busch	22	18 percent
2. Schlitz	15	12 percent
3. Pabst	10	8 percent
4. Coors	7	6 percent
5. Schaefer	6	5 percent

1980: The Top Five Brewing Companies		
1. Anheuser-Busch	50	28 percent
2. Miller	37	21 percent
3. Pabst	15	9 percent
4. Schlitz	15	9 percent
5. Coors	14	8 percent

THE EVOLUTION OF AMERICA'S TOP BREWING COMPANIES
(in Millions of Barrels sold in the US Market)

1990: The Top Five Brewing Companies	Annual Output	Share of Total
1. Anheuser-Busch	80	42 percent
2. Miller	61	22 percent
3. Stroh	21	10 percent
4. Coors	20	9 percent
5. Heileman	19	8 percent

2000: The Top Ten Brewing Companies		
1. Anheuser-Busch	98.3	53.42 percent
2. Miller	41.6	22.60 percent
3. Coors	23.0	12.50 percent
4. Pabst	10.5	5.70 percent
5. Genesee	1.4	.07 percent
6. Boston Beer	1.2	.06 percent
7. Latrobe	1.2	.06 percent
8. D.G. Yuengling	.9	.05 percent
9. Sierra Nevada	.5	.03 percent
10. Minnesota	.4	.02 percent

THE TOP TEN UNITED STATES BREWING COMPANIES AT THE TURN OF THE CENTURY
(in Millions of Barrels sold in the US Market)
(The 1990 ranking and output are in parentheses; the final figure is percentage of change from 1990 to 2000)

1.(1) Anheuser-Busch	98.3	(86.5)	13.6
2.(2) Miller	41.6	(43.5)	-4.4
3.(3) Coors	23.0	(19.2)	19.8
4.(6) Pabst	10.5	(6.3)	66.7
5.(7) Genesee	1.4	(2.2)	-38.6
6.(15) Boston Beer	1.2	(.1)	1008.0
7.(9) Latrobe	1.2	(.7)	60.8
8.(14) D.G. Yuengling	.9	(.1)	569.6
9.(30) Sierra Nevada	.5	(.03)	1509.6
10. Minnesota	.4		[No Data]

FOREIGN IMPORTS INTO THE UNITED STATES AT THE TURN OF THE CENTURY
(by Country and Millions of Barrels)

1. Mexico (Mainly Modelo)	6.7
2. Netherlands (Mainly Heineken)	4.4
3. Canada	3.1
4. Germany	1.2
5. Ireland (Mainly Guinness)	0.8
6. United Kingdom	0.8
7. Japan	0.1

(The total beer imports into the United States at the turn of the century stood at 18 million barrels annually.)

ANNUAL OUTPUT AND MARKET SHARE OF THE TOP TEN UNITED STATES BREWING COMPANIES AT THE TURN OF THE CENTURY
(in Millions of Barrels sold in the US Market)

1. Anheuser-Busch	98.3	53.42 percent
2. Miller	41.6	22.60 percent
3. Coors	23.0	12.50 percent
4. Pabst	10.5	5.70 percent
5. Genesee	1.4	.07 percent
6. Boston Beer	1.2	.06 percent
7. Latrobe	1.2	.06 percent
8. D.G. Yuengling	.9	.05 percent
9. Sierra Nevada	.5	.03 percent
10. Minnesota	.4	.02 percent

(Minnesota Brewing closed its doors in 2002, with its flagship brand, Grain Belt, being acquired by August Schell.)

ANNUAL OUTPUT AND MARKET SHARE OF THE TOP TEN UNITED STATES BREWING COMPANIES IN 2005
(in Millions of Barrels sold in the US Market)

1. Anheuser-Busch	101.1	49.47 percent
2. Miller	38.6	18.74 percent
3. Coors	22.1	11.08 percent
4. Pabst	11.1	3.38 percent
5. D.G. Yuengling	1.6	.08 percent
6. Boston Beer	1.4	.07 percent
7. City Brewery (LaCrosse)	1.0	.05 percent
8. Latrobe	.9	.05 percent
9. High Falls	.7	.03 percent
10. Sierra Nevada	.6	.03 percent

ANNUAL OUTPUT OF THE SECOND TIER (BEGINNING WITH NUMBER ELEVEN) UNITED STATES BREWING COMPANIES AT THE TURN OF THE CENTURY
(in Millions of Barrels sold in the US Market)

Leinenkugel Brewing	331,000***	Hops Restaurants	26,723 ****
Matt Brewing	276,000	Old Dominion Brewing	26,640
Pittsburgh Brewing	275,000	Magic Hat Brewing	26,100
Spoetzl Brewery	261,727	City Brewery	25,550
Redhook Ale Brewery	212,600	Kalamazoo Brewing	24,657
New Belgium Brewing	164,800	Otter Creek Brewing	24,492
Pete's Brewing	151,975 *	Pennsylvania Brewing	22,000
Widmer Brothers	127,000	Odell Brewing	20,592
Pyramid Breweries	109,945	McMenamin's	19,588 ****
Anchor Brewing	97,000	Rogue Ales	19,300
Deschutes Brewing	95,272	Utah Brewers	18,011
Alaskan Brewing	83,354	Great Lakes Brewing	17,927
Portland Brewing	68,209	Rockies Brewing	17,852
Full Sail Brewing	64,884	Anderson Valley	17,731
Gordon Biersch	60,237 ****	Big Sky Brewing	17,200
Joseph Huber Brewing	60,000	Golden Pacific	16,129
Mass Bay Brewing	53,100	D.L. Geary Brewing	15,822
Stevens Point	50,000	Celis Brewery	15,070
Mendocino Brewing	49,255	Lagunitas Brewing	14,809
Dixie Brewing	46,000	North Coast Brewing	14,639
Jones Brewing	43,380	Sprecher Brewing	14,118
Goose Island	43,000	Uinta Brewing	13,749
Summit Brewing	42,904	Capital Brewery	13,369
Hudepohl-Schoenling	40,676	Hale's Ales	13,220
Boulevard Brewing	39,339		
Straub Brewing	36,041		
Abita Brewing	34,500		
Brooklyn Brewery	31,906		
Shipyard Brewery	30,985		
BridgePort Brewing	30,720		
Frederick Brewing	29,772		
August Schell	27,700		

* Indicates a "contract" brewer whose beer is produced at another brewery.
** Indicates a brewery whose totals include some "Contract" brewed beer.
*** Leinenkugel is a wholly-owned subsidiary of Miller Brewing, but the data is shown separately in this table because Leinenkugel is treated as a separate operating unit.
**** Gordon Biersch, McMenamin's and Hops are chains of brewpubs and brewery restaurants.

THE LEADING UNITED STATES BREWING COMPANIES IN 2005

(With their 2005 domestic production data in 31-gallon barrels)

Anheuser-Busch	St. Louis, Missouri	101,100,000	Anchor Brewing	San Francisco, CA	83,062	
Miller Brewing	Milwaukee, Wisconsin	38,300,000*	August Schell	New Ulm, Minnesota	69,882	
Adolph Coors	Golden, Colorado	22,645,000*	Magic Hat Brewing	Burlington, Vermont	60,888	
Pabst Brewing	Milwaukee, Wisconsin	6,900,000	Bell's Brewery	Galesburg, Michigan	57,360	
D.G. Yuengling	Pottsville, Pennsylvania	1,570,000	Shipyard Brewery	Portland, Maine	56,151	
Boston Beer Company	Boston, Massachusetts	1,400,000	Brooklyn Brewery	Brooklyn, New York	53,200	
City Brewery	LaCrosse, Wisconsin	1,005,793	Mammoth Brewing	Mammoth Lakes, CA	52,142	
Latrobe Brewing	Latrobe, Pennsylvania	990,000	Abita Brewing	Abita Springs, LA	52,000	
High Falls	Rochester, New York	705,000	BridgePort Brewing	Portland, Oregon	43,432	
Sierra Nevada	Chico, California	612,640	Rogue Ales	Newport, Oregon	43,000	
Pittsburgh	Pittsburgh, Pennsylvania	365,000	Rock Bottom	Louisville, Colorado	41,830***	
New Belgium Brewing	Fort Collins, Colorado	350,000	New Glarus	New Glarus, Wisconsin	39,662	
Mackenzie River	San Francisco, California	350,000	Firestone-Walker	Paso Robles, California	38,450	
Leinenkugel Brewing	Chippewa Falls, Wisconsin	340,000**	Stone Brewing	Escondido, California	36,394	
Spoetzl Brewery	Shiner, Texas	299,727	Straub Brewing	St. Mary's, Pennsylvania	34,000	
Matt Brewing	Utica, New York	251,800	Great Lakes Brewing	Cleveland, Ohio	33,633	
Redhook Ale Brewery	Seattle, Washington	234,200	Lagunitas Brewing	Lagunitas, California	32,420	
Pyramid Breweries	Kalama, Washington	230,500***	Mac & Jack's	Redmond, Washington	30,589	
Widmer Brothers	Portland, Oregon	226,500	Dogfish Head	Milton, Delaware	29,750	
Joseph Huber Brewing	Monroe, Wisconsin	189,000	Odell Brewing	Fort Collins, Colorado	28,830	
Deschutes Brewing	Bend, Oregon	144,422	Big Sky Brewing	Missoula, Montana	28,800	
Alaskan Brewing	Juneau, Alaska	105,300	Dixie Brewing	New Orleans, Louisiana	28,000	
Boulevard Brewing	Kansas City, Missouri	103,584	Old Dominion	Ashburn, Virginia	27,517	
Mass Bay Brewing	Boston, Massachusetts	90,333	BJ's Restaurants	Huntington Beach, CA	25,536***	
Carolina Beer	Mooresville, NC	87,105	Lost Coast Brewery	Eureka, California	24,405	
Full Sail Brewing	Hood River, Oregon	85,756	Victory Brewing	Downington, PA	23,800	

NOTES:

Of the top four, Anheuser-Busch and Miller operate multiple breweries across the United States, Coors operates two and Pabst operates none — contracting out 100 percent of its production. The location given for these multi-site operators and for the brewpub chains (***) is that of their corporate headquarters.

In 2002 Miller was acquired by London-based South African Breweries (SAB) to form SABMiller, and in 2005, Coors merged with Molson Breweries of Canada to form Molson Coors Brewing.

* Both Miller and Coors are part of international conglomerates.

** Subsidiary of Miller Brewing

*** Brewery Restaurant chain

**** Total includes Portland Brewing which merged with Pyramid.

Source: Modern Brewery Age

Index

Abita Brewing 128, 155-156

Acme Brewing 80-81, 83, 94-95, 97, 99

Adams, Joseph 13

Adams, Samuel (beer brand, see also Boston Beer) 109, 123-124, 128, 134-135

Adams, Samuel (person) 13

Adel, Iowa 123

Alaskan Brewing 137, 155-156

Albany 39, 89, 118, 125

Albatross Saloon 119

Alberta 77-78, 137

Alexander, James 10

Allentown 89-90

Alloway Tavern 21

Alsace 152

Altbier 120, 144

Amarillo 144

American Brewer 19

American Revolution 11, 15, 82

American Society of Brewing Chemists 7

Amsterdam Amber 124

Anchor Brewing 4, 29, 60, 115-116, 118-119, 121-122, 142, 152, 155-156

Anchor Steam Beer 116

Anderson Valley Brewing 155

Anheuser, Eberhard 47, 51

Anheuser-Busch 43, 46-50, 56, 71, 74, 77-78, 85-87, 90, 95, 98, 101, 105, 107, 111-112, 113, 126-127, 131, 133, 136, 141, 154-156

Anti-Saloon League 68-69

Appalachian Mountains 21, 24

Arizona 6-7

Aspen 57, 140

Association of Brewers 138

Atlanta 100

Augsberger 122

August Schell 108-109, 121-122, 155-156

Austin, Mary 93

B.J.'s 139, 156

Badenhausen, Carl 76, 84

Bain, Robin 92

Baldwinsville 87, 105

Ballantine, family and brewery 38-41, 74-76, 89-91, 102, 104, 129, 154

Baltimore 11, 24, 62, 68, 89, 98, 100, 153

Banks, Emily 93

Baron, Stanley 75, 85-87, 89, 105, 116-117, 142

Baruth, Ernst 60

Bayard, Balthazar 9

Beehrer, Charles 58

Behloradsky, J.B. 56

Belleville 79, 100, 106, 109

Bend, Oregon 133-134, 137-138, 156

Bensonville 79

Berghoff 137

Best, family and breweries 13-14, 19-20, 24, 30-33, 42-43, 59

Betzold 56

Biersch, Dean 138

Big Eddy Springs 34

Big Sky Brewing 155-156

Bigfoot Ale 119

Blatz, Valentin and brewery 30, 33-34, 44, 46, 68, 87, 90, 107, 129

Blitz-Weinhard Brewery 87, 95, 99, 109, 128-129

Blumer Brewery 137

Bock Beer 25-26, 128, 144-146, 149

Bohemia 149-150, 152

Bohemian Distributing Company 81

Bond, Alan 109, 127

Boston Beer Company 123-124, 128, 133-135, 140-141, 154-156

Boston 9, 13, 15, 27, 68, 123-126, 128, 133-135, 140-141, 146, 154-156

Boulder Brewing 117-118, 128, 139, 141

Boulevard Brewing 4, 137-138, 142, 155-156

Bourke, John 6

Braun, Johann 46

Brekle, Gottlieb 29, 60

Breweriana 145

Brewers Association 125, 139, 141, 146, 150-151

Brewing Corporation of America 100

Brewpubs 119-120, 124, 130-131, 134, 137-139, 146, 155-156

Briant, Samuel 11

BridgePort Brewing 155-156

Brooklyn Brewery 124, 136, 155-156

Brooklyn 18, 38, 40-42, 74, 86, 88-89, 91

Buckeye Brewery 54

Budweiser 47, 49-50, 74, 111, 122, 137

Buffalo Brewing 128

Bull, William 28

Burgermeister 87, 101

Burnett, John 7

Busch, Adolphus Busch 18, 46-47, 49, 51, 56, 105, 126

California Brewing Association 60, 81

California 26-29, 42, 59-60, 81, 83, 86-87, 94-95, 99, 114, 118, 120, 126, 128, 130, 134, 137-138, 140, 144, 152, 156

Campbell-Mithun 96-97

Camusi, Paul 118, 134

Canada 77, 79, 99-101, 109, 111-112, 119, 123, 127, 132, 135, 137, 144, 146, 148-149, 155-156

Cannon, James 70

Capital Brewery 155

Capital Brewing 59

Capone, Al 71, 79

Carling and Carling O'Keefe companies 79, 99-101, 107, 109

Carolina Beer 156

Carpenter, Mark 4

Carre, Ferdinand 41

Catamount Brewing 125

Cedar Brewing 123

Celebration Ale 118-119

Celis Brewery 155

Centennial Brewery 58-59

Century Brewing 77

Charlotte 47

Chicago 25, 31, 35, 42-44, 46, 53, 79-80, 87, 105, 107

Christen, Joseph 55

Cincinnati 23-24, 26, 50, 54, 59, 109, 134

City Brewery (LaCrosse) 135-136, 155-156

City Brewery 26, 29, 34, 46

Civil War 20, 24-27, 35-36, 46, 55, 59, 62-63, 66, 70, 73, 121

Cleveland 66, 85, 89, 100-101

Coeur d'Alene Brewing 132

Colorado 7, 30, 56-57, 71, 103, 112, 117-118, 128, 132, 137, 139-141, 156

Columbus 6, 62, 71, 146, 153

Congress Beer 40

Conrad, Carl 48

Consumers Brewing Company 52

Coors, family and brewery 4, 57, 71, 111-112, 125, 127, 130, 132-133, 141, 154-156

Coppinger, Joseph 17-20

Cox, Rowland 49

Crown Cork 62

Curtis, Edward 7

D'Addona, Robert 124-125

Dallas County Brewing 123

Darrow, Madelyn 92

Davis, John 31

Deschutes Brewery 133-134, 137-138, 155-156

Detroit 54

Diversey, Michael 25

Dixie Brewing 55-56, 155-156

Dock Street 10, 124-125

Dogfish Head Brewery 132, 156

Double Barrel 128

DuBois Brewery 49

Duyn, Kate 133, 137

Eagle Brewery 21, 31

Ehret, George 37-38, 41-42, 74, 86

Emlen family and brewery 10, 14

Empire Brewery 28, 32-33

England 6, 8-13, 16, 21, 24-25, 38, 126, 144, 146-148, 150, 152

Eureka Brewing 109

Evans, George 15

Falkenburg, Jinx 91, 93

Falls City 108

Falstaff Brewing 4, 50-52, 66, 73, 78-79, 85-87, 95, 100-104, 129, 154

Falstaff, Sir John 50-51

Fat Tire Amber 137, 139

Feigenspan Brewery 29, 90

Figge family 96-97, 99

Finkel, Charles 4

Fire Rock Pale Ale 140

Firestone Walker 128, 156

Fish, Gary 133, 138

Fisher Brewing Company 96

Fisher's, T.W. 132

Fleckenstein Brothers Brewery 26

Fleischbein 47

Fleishman Bavarian Brewery 24

Flying Dog Brewery 140

Forest Park Brewing Company 52

Fort Bragg 120, 140

Fort Collins 137, 139, 156

Fort Pitt 10

Fort Worth 100, 132

Fortmann, Franz 24, 26

Foto, J.S. 81

Frampton, William 10

Frankenmuth 100

Frederick Brewing 155

Full Sail Brewing 132, 134, 155-156

Fuller, John 18

Gatza, Paul 141

Gavin, Ernie 97

Geary Brewing 125-126, 155

General Brewing 81, 95, 102-104

Genesee Brewing (see also High Falls) 133, 135, 154-155

Georgia 10-11, 87, 100

Gerber, George 78

Germany and Germans 16, 21-26,
    29-33, 38, 44, 46-47, 49-52, 54,
    56, 60, 68, 70-71, 76, 120, 123,
    126, 134, 142, 144-153, 155
Germany 126, 145-148, 152-153
Gillig, George 24
Gintz, Peter 79
Gipfel, David 31, 44
Girl-in-the-Moon 127
Gluek, family and breweries 26, 60,
    81
Golden Pacific 155
Goose Island 155
Gordon Biersch 138, 140-141, 155
Gordon, Dan 4, 138
Gottlieb-Bauernschmidt-Straus
    Brewing 68
Goulding, Ray 97
Gover, Sonia 92
Grace, W.R. Company 101
Grain Belt 26, 52, 54, 107, 128, 155
Grant, Bert 118-119
Great American Beer Festival 122,
    138
Great Falls Breweries 78
Great Lakes Brewing 155-156
Griesedieck family and breweries
    51-52, 78-79, 85-86, 100, 104,
    106, 109
Grossman, Ken 118, 134
Guinness 16, 17, 101, 152, 155
Gulf Brewing 98, 101
Gund, John 34, 135
Gundlach, Jacob 28
Gunther Brewing 98, 153
Haberle 40
Haffenreffer Brewery 123, 134
Half Moon Bay Brewing 130
Hamilton, Alexander 16-17, 20
Hamm family and brewery 26, 52,
    54, 71, 79-80, 87, 95-99, 101-102,
    104, 115, 129, 145
Hammer, Phillip 47
Hansen National Brewery 81

Hansen, Charles 60
Hare, Robert 14-15
Harpoon Brewing 125-126
Hart Brewing 137
Harvard University 9
Harwood, Ralph 14
Hawaii Brewing 89, 140
Hawaii 89, 139-141, 152
Healy, Cameron 140
Heartland Brewing 130
Heidelberg 129
Heileman family and brewery 34,
    105-109, 127-131, 133, 135, 154
Heineken 131, 155
Heinrich Brewing 52
Hell Gate Brewery 37-38
Hemrich, Andrew 59
Heublein 99, 101
Heurich family 124
High Falls Brewing (see also
    Genesee) 135, 155-156
Highlander 58, 78, 99-100
Hillsdale Brewery 119
Hitchner, George 21
Hoffman Beverage 86-87
Honolulu Brewing 139
Honolulu 89, 139-141
Hood River 132, 134, 156
Hopland 119-120
Hops Restaurants 139, 155
Horton, William 11
Houston 87, 98, 101
Hovel, Cleo 96
Howard, William 18
Huber Brewing 137, 155-156
Hudepohl, family and brewery 52,
    54, 109
Hudepohl-Schoenling 109, 134, 155
Hupfel, Anton 37
Idaho 132, 148
Illinois 11, 57, 74, 79, 85, 100, 105-
    106, 109, 122
InBev (formerly Interbrew) 123,
    131, 136

Independent Brewing 68
Indiana 86, 122, 126, 147
Interstate Brewing Company 95
Issleib, Lutz 129
Jackson Brewing 56, 97
Jax (see Jackson Brewing)
Jeff Lebesch, Jeff 137, 139
Jeff Ware, Jeff 124
Jefferson, Thomas 13, 17-20, 70
Jones Brewing 108-110, 155
Jordan, Kim 137, 139
Kalamazoo Brewing 155
Kalmanovitz, Paul 102-103, 105,
    129
Kansas City 86, 106, 137, 142, 156
Katz, Solomon 7
Keller, Andrew 26, 52
Kemper, Thomas Brewing 137
Kentucky 25, 49, 126
Kessler, family and brewery 50, 58,
    125
Khalsa, Spoon 140
Knickerbocker 75
Koch, Jim 109, 123-124, 128, 133-134
Koethe Brewery 31
Kolb, Charles 90
Kona Brewing 140-141
Koolau 140
Kopp, John 59
Kotte, George 54
Kroenke, Henry 60
Krueger Brewing 73
Krug, Anna 44
Krug, August 44
Krug, Fred 79
Kuhn, Christopher 29
Labatt Brewing 112, 123, 135-136,
    148
LaCrosse 34, 128, 135-136, 155-156
Lagunitas Brewing 140, 155-156
Lake Brewery 31
Lakefront Brewery 122
Latrobe Brewing 122-123, 135-136,
    156

Lear, Tobias 14
Leinenkugel Brewing 34, 110, 137,
    155-156
Lemp, family and brewery 50-52
Lethbridge Brewery 77-78, 99
Levis, Mike 131
Liebman, Walter (Terry) 4, 133, 136
Liebmann, family and brewery 4,
    40-41, 91-92, 94-95, 133, 136
Lill, William 25
Lincoln, Abraham 121
Lion Brewery 9, 54
Lite (brand) 111-112
Lone Star Brewery 56, 105-107, 109
Los Angeles 29, 81, 86, 94-96, 98,
    101, 103
Lost Coast Brewery 126, 156
Louisiana 128, 156
Lucky Lager 80-81, 94-96, 99, 102-
    103, 129
Lutz, H. F. 7-8
Mack, Jacob 57
Mack, John 57
Mackenzie River 156
Mad Anthony 126
Magic Hat Brewing 155-156
Maier Brewing 103
Maier, J.R. 31
Maine 125-126, 156
Mammoth Brewing 156
Man Full O'Trouble 10, 12
Manger, George 23
Manhattan Brewing 124
Manhattan 9, 13, 38, 42, 74-75,
    124-125
Marco, Dani 137
Maryland 89
Mass Bay Brewing 125, 155-156
Massachusetts Breweries 68
Massachusetts 8-9, 13, 68, 100, 156
Matt Brewing 124-125, 136-137,
    155-156
Maui 140-141
Mayflower 8

Maytag, Fritz 115-118, 121, 142
McAuliffe, Jack 118
McMenamin, family and breweries
    119, 138-139, 155
Meisterbrau 87
Melms, C.J. 31
Melsheimer, Max 57
Memphis 87, 105
Mendocino Brewing 119-120, 155
Menomenee Valley Brewery 32
Menominee Brewery 31
Menominee River Brewing 68
Merrit, Hillie 92
Mertz, George 55
Mexico 7, 26, 67, 131, 152, 155
Michelob 50, 112
Michigan 68, 78, 107, 122, 156
Microbreweries 117-119, 121, 124-
    126, 132-140, 144, 146, 150, 152
Miller, Ernst 66
Miller, Frederick and brewery 4, 32,
    34, 40, 62, 63, 66-68, 101-102,
    110-111, 113, 122, 127-128, 155-
    156
Miller, John 32, 34
Milwaukee 9, 27-28, 30-35, 37, 42-
    44, 46, 51-52, 57, 60, 62-63, 66-
    68, 70-71, 82, 85, 87-88, 101-102,
    104-105, 107
Minneapolis 26, 52, 107, 122
Minnesota Brewing Company 107,
    128, 155
Minnesota 26, 52, 96-97, 107-109,
    121-122, 128, 154-156
Mirror Pond Pale Ale 138
Miss Rheingold 31-94, 115, 133,
    136-137
Mississippi (river and state) 11, 25-
    28, 34, 50, 52, 55, 79, 89
Missoula 78, 99-100
Missouri 46, 86, 106, 114, 137, 156
Mitaro, Mike 136
Mithun, Ray 96
Modelo 155

Moerlein, Christian 53-54
Molson Breweries 99, 127, 156
Molson Coors Brewing 132, 156
Montana Beverages 58, 125
Montana 57-58, 77-78, 96, 99, 125,
    130, 132, 156
Morris, Benjamin 13
Mound City 79
Mount Holly 10, 13
Mountain Brewing Company 57
Mountain Crest Brewing 137
Muehlebach Brewing 86, 106
Mueller, Henry 59
Naperville 57
Narragansett Brewery 102, 104
National Breweries 18-19, 51-52,
    60, 81, 94
National Brewing 79
Near Beer 71, 150, 154
Nebraska 79
Neu, Philip 79
Neukirch, Franz 31
New Albion Brewing 118
New Belgium Brewing 137, 139-
    140, 155-156
New England 8, 104, 126
New Glarus 156
New Hampshire 87
New Jersey 13, 21, 39, 74, 86, 136
New Mexico 131
New Orleans 25, 55-56, 63, 68, 85,
    97, 104
New York City 12, 20, 33, 35, 37-
    43, 46, 63, 68, 74-75, 89-90, 93-
    94, 97, 124-125, 130, 137
New York 10, 12, 14, 18, 20, 23-24,
    28-29, 33-35, 37-43, 46, 52, 63-
    64, 68, 74-77, 85-87, 89-91, 93-
    94, 97, 114, 118, 123-125, 128-
    130, 133, 136-137, 156
Newark 39-40, 42, 73, 86, 90-91
Newman, Paul 93
Newman, William 118, 125
Newport 140, 150, 156

Noerenberg Brewing 52
North Carolina 11, 47, 87
North Coast Brewing 94, 120, 140, 155
North Star Brewery 26
Obermeyer, David 41
Odell Brewing 155-156
Ohio 66, 70, 85, 87, 89, 100, 156
Old Dominion Brewing 155, 156
Old Fashion of Billings 58
Olde Heurich Brewing 124
Oldenberg Brewery 126
Olympia, city and brewery 58-59, 98-99, 102, 104, 107, 109, 111, 129-130, 145
Omaha 79, 85, 104
Oregon 4, 26-27, 29, 71, 77-78, 87, 95-96, 119-120, 132-134, 136-138, 140, 144, 146, 148, 156
Orth, John 26, 52
Otter Creek Brewing 126, 155
Owens, Buffalo Bill 119
Owens, Richard 31
Owens, Richard 31
Ownbey, Ruth 92
Pabst, Frederick and brewery 9, 30, 32-34, 37, 42-44, 46, 55, 61, 66, 68, 71, 73-74, 85-87, 95, 102-105, 107, 128-130, 132-133, 135, 154-156
Pacific Brewing 141
Page, James 122
Palisade Brewery 74
Pastorius, Tom 124
Patterson, Erastus 39
Paul, A.C. 67
Paul, Allan 4, 119
Pawlett, William 31
Pawnee Dark 62
Pearl Brewing 56, 130, 132
Penn, William 10, 12
Pennsylvania Brewing 155
Pennsylvania 7, 10, 12, 21, 33, 35, 49, 68, 89, 108-109, 121-124, 128, 135-137, 155-156

Pepper, Henry 17
Pfeiffer, Heinrich 17
Philadelphia 10, 12-15, 17, 23-24, 28, 46, 60, 93, 123-125
Philip Morris 101, 130
Phoenix Brewery 46
Phoenix 100
Piel Brothers Brewing 97, 129
Pilsner 22, 49, 113, 122, 124-125, 131, 147, 150
Pittsburgh 10, 17, 26, 68, 109, 124-125, 137, 155-156
Pittsburgh Brewing 68, 109, 137, 155, 156
Plank Road Brewery 32-33, 127
Portland 4, 29, 87, 95, 99, 109, 119-120, 125-126, 128-129, 136-138, 155-156
Portland Brewing 137, 155-156
Prohibition 11, 24, 49, 51-52, 54, 56-57, 59-60, 70, 71, 73, 116-117, 119, 121, 144, 146, 150-151, 154
Pyramid Breweries 137, 155-156
Rabbeson, A.B. 59
Raddant, Emil 44
Rainier Breweries 59, 77-81, 97, 99, 108-109, 128-129
Rathe Washington Brewery 28
Red Cap Ale 101, 109
Red Lion Brewery 9
Redhook Brewery 118, 121, 131, 137, 155-156
Regional Craft Brewery 151
Reinheitsgebot 123, 151
Repeal of Prohibition 70, 72-74, 76-77, 79, 81, 116, 151
Reuthlisberger, Herman 31
Rheingold (see also Liebmann and Miss Rheingold) 91-94, 99, 115, 133, 136-137
Rhode Island 10, 104
Riedelschoefer 31
Riedlingen 33
River City Brewing 118

Rock Bottom Restaurants 139, 156
Rockies Brewing 117-118, 155
Rocky Mountain Brewery 30, 57
Rogue Ales 140, 155-156
Rolling Rock 123, 135-136
Roosevelt, Franklin 72
Rossmarck, George 24
Rost, George 24
Roth, Carl 103
Ruedrich, Mark 4
Ruppert, Jacob and brewery 39, 74-75, 77, 89, 91
Rutgers, Henry 12
Ryder, David 7
S & P 103, 104
SAB and SABMiller 130-132, 156
Salem Brewery 78, 100
Salt Lake City 96, 102
San Antonio 26, 46, 56, 105-106, 130
San Antonio Brewing 56
San Diego 60
San Francisco 4, 27-29, 46, 59-60, 63, 78, 81, 86-87, 94-95, 97, 101-102, 104, 116, 118-119, 130, 142, 152, 156
San Francisco Brewing 119, 130
San Jose 86, 95
Santa Fe Brewing 131
Saxer, Henry 29
Schaefer, family and brewery 24, 38, 41, 74-76, 88-91, 98, 129, 154
Schalk Brothers 40
Schandien, Emil 33
Schell Brewing, see August Schell
Schinkel, Otto 60
Schirf Brewing 128
Schliebitz, Herman 32
Schlitz, Joseph and Schlitz Brewing 30, 34, 42-44, 46, 55, 62, 66, 68, 71, 73-74, 82-83, 85-90, 95, 101, 105, 107, 111, 114, 127, 130, 140, 154
Schmidt, family and breweries 58-59, 107-108, 128-129, 131

Schneider, George 47-48, 50
Schueler, Jacob 57
Schuppert, Adam 28
Schwechat Brewery 22
Seattle 59, 76-78, 99-100, 109, 118, 128-129, 131, 137, 156
Seattle Brewing and Malting 59, 77-78, 99
Shiner Brewing 56, 137, 156
Shipman, Paul 118
Shipyard Brewery 155-156
Sick, family and breweries 76-78, 99-100, 109
Siebel Institute of Technology 144
Sierra Nevada Brewing 115, 118-119, 133-135, 140-141, 154-156
Sisk, Michael 10
Solomon, F.Z. 30
Sommers, Sebastian 38
South African Breweries (see also SABMiller) 130-131, 156
Specht, Jacob 28
Spoetzl Brewery 56, 137, 155-156
Spokane 77-78, 99-100
St. Clair 133
St. Louis 42, 46-47, 50-52, 59, 66, 68, 77-78, 85, 100, 104, 109, 136, 156
St. Louis Brewing Association 51-52, 68
St. Paul 25-26, 52, 79, 96, 107, 122, 128
St. Vincent 122-123
Stag 53, 79, 100, 106, 108-109, 129
Stanislaus Brewing 120
Stenger Brewery 57
Stevens Point, town and brewery 18, 109, 122-123, 155
Stifel, Otto 78
Stone Brewing 156
Stoney's Beer 108-109
Stoudt Brewing 128
Straub Brewing 155-156

Stroh family and brewery 54-55, 67, 71, 90, 105, 107, 111, 122, 127-130, 133, 135, 154
Stumpf, Wilhelm 47, 50
Stuyvesant, Peter 9-10
Summit Brewing 122, 155
Swan Brewery 109
Tacoma 100
Tampa 87, 105, 133
Tennessee 25, 87
Texas 26, 55-56, 86-87, 98, 106-108, 130, 132, 137, 156
Three Tun Tavern 10, 13
Tivoli (Tivoli Union) Brewery 56, 57, 151
Triple Rock 131
Tuborg 108
Tumwater 58-59, 98-99, 102, 104, 129-131
Twenty Tank 130
Uihlein, August 44
Uihlein, Henry 88
Uinta Brewing 155
Union Brewery 31, 56
Union City 74
US Brewers Foundation 101, 105, 142
Utah 128, 155
Utica 124, 136-137, 156
Van Buren, Martin 20
Vancouver 29, 95, 104
Vassar, family, college and brewery 20-21
Vaughn, Sharon 94, 133
Vermont 125-126, 156
Victory Brewing 156
Vincennes, Indiana 147
Virginia City 29, 57
Virginia 8-9, 11, 13-14, 31, 87, 156
Vitale, Frank 81
Volstead Act 71
Wagner, Johan 23, 31
Waimea Brewing 140
Walter Brewing Company 103

Washington Brewery 28, 59
Washington 4, 13-20, 26, 28-30, 58-59, 70, 77, 82, 95, 99-100, 102, 104, 107, 118, 124, 130-131, 137-138, 142, 156
Washington, George 4, 13-17, 19, 70, 82, 142
Wechsler, Bob 91
Weinhard, Henry and brewery (see also Blitz) 29, 71, 108, 128-129, 131-132
Weiss Beer Brewery 32
West End Brewing 124
Western Breweries 26, 51, 79, 106
Widmer, family and brewery 120, 136-138, 155-156
Wieland, John 60
Wiessner, family and brewery 24
Wilmot, Charles 60
Wilson, Bob 141
Winston-Salem 87, 105, 129
Wisconsin 21, 30, 32, 34, 40, 42, 107-110, 120, 122, 128, 130, 135, 137, 156
Wittemann Company 64
Wolaver 126
World War I 71, 82, 84, 87, 89, 105
World War II 74-75, 81-82, 84, 86, 94-95, 111, 117, 126, 145
Wurttemberg 21, 33
Yakima Brewing 118
Yakima 118-119, 144
Yoerg, Anton and brewery 26, 52
Yuengling, family and brewery 21, 33, 109, 121-122, 133, 141, 154-156
Zahler, Anton 52
Zang, Philip 57
Zhouging, China 104

Above: Friends enjoying a few beers in the warmth of the Sportsmen's Tavern on a rainy day in November 1940. (*Library of Congress*)